Cars of the World in Colour

SPORTS CARS
1907–1927

by
T. R. NICHOLSON

Illustrated by
JOHN W. WOOD

Norman Dinnage
Frank Friend
Brian Hiley
William Hobson
Tony Mitchell
Jack Pelling

LONDON
BLANDFORD PRESS

First published in 1970
copyright © 1970 Blandford Press Ltd.
167 High Holborn, London WCιV 6PH
ISBN 0 7137 60029

O 7137 OO 629

ACKNOWLEDGEMENTS

The author and publishers are grateful to the following for their help and advice
in the preparation of this book, and for checking the manuscript: Mr Angelo
Tito Anselmi; Lt.-Col. C. H. D. Berthon; Mr Charles L. Betts Jr; Mr H. G.
Conway; Mr Bernard de Lassée; Mr D. C. Field; Mr G. N. Georgano; Mr
Antony Hannoyer; Mr Egon Hanus; Mr Peter Hull; Mr Lucien Loreille; Ing
Norberto Pedroso; Mr. Jackie Pichon; Mr Cyril Posthumus; Mr Michael
Sedgwick; Dr Alfred Waldis.

Colour section printed by Colour Reproduction Ltd. Billericay
Text printed in Great Britain by
Richard Clay (The Chaucer Press) Ltd, Bungay, Suffolk

INTRODUCTION

In the Introduction to the volume on *Sports Cars 1928–1939* in this series, a brief outline of the earlier history of the breed was provided. The writer will try to avoid too much repetition now, though a certain amount is unavoidable.

The sports car did not begin in one place or grow from one root. This would be an impossibility if only because the name means different things to different people. This book tries to cover all the more familiar definitions, tracing the development of each type, in an attempt to satisfy the greatest number of readers, and also for the reason that any narrow, exclusive definition is hard to justify.

Some people hold that a sports car is any dual-purpose machine, suited either to competition or to normal road use. Thus, we should include cars that were deliberate compromises—neither one thing nor the other, nor any identifiable type at all. They were either basically touring machines with slight bodywork and (perhaps) tuned engines; or cars that were fundamentally racers, made tractable and more civilized for road use. Such vehicles antedated the sports cars in their own right, and until the First World War were made alongside them. Examples shown here are confined to those that were contemporary with their more specialized brethren: the Cottin et Desgouttes from France (6), and the Isotta-Fraschini Tipo KM from Italy (8).

Unlike that of Europe, the sports car (or more properly, sport car) of America was neither evolved from nor intended for competitions in any shape or form. The purpose of the speedster was to invest its driver with an air of sportiness in general; not to imbue it or the man at its wheel with anything suggestive of motor sport in particular. It was a suitable vehicle to carry him to his golf, sailing, riding, flying or other pursuits. So its lines were rakish and elegant in the extreme, but its handling qualities might be no improvement on those of the touring car in the catalogue from which it was usually derived, and its performance was better only because its extremely sketchy bodies meant less weight and allowed higher gearing. There was no call for technical sophistication or high efficiency, so the same type of large, leisurely engine seen in the touring model was often found in the speedster. The latter was indeed a specialized vehicle, but only in the sense that its bodywork made it totally impracticable for anything except its function as a rich man's fine-weather toy. Probably its purpose was best summed up in the name of the sporting Stanley —the Gentleman's Speedy Roadster (11). A short trip to the links or the marina in a car usually consisting of little more than two seats, four wings and a hood on an otherwise bare chassis was tolerable; twenty-four hours of continuous high-speed slog in all weathers around the Le Mans circuit in France or the Spa circuit in Belgium demanded something more habitable. Of course the same cars, or hotter versions of them, could and did win races for stock cars, since few of the latter could live with the Mercer

Fig. 1. Sizaire-Naudin front suspension, France, *c.* 1938 (see 5)

Type 35 (13), the 50 h.p. Lozier (12) or the Stutz Bearcat (14); in their own *milieu* they could be serious competition machines, if only incidentally.

The passage of time, and the increasing tendency to conform and to seek comfort that was visible not only in the United States but all over the world, served to tame the speedsters. By the early 1920s, they had more comfortable bodies; they were heavier, lower-geared, and (most of them) less exciting. The two types of Stutz illustrated point the contrast. As the decade wore on, the market for individualists' cars like the speedster declined, and by 1927 all but a handful had gone. The Kissel (32) was one of the longest lived and most distinguished. Some of the other survivors were to enjoy an Indian summer of fame, for the first time providing formidable competition for established European makes at Le Mans, though disappearing from stock car racing at home.

The European sports car in most, if not all, possible definitions of the term was unarguably derived from and encouraged by competitions from its beginnings. In contrast with America, the Latin nations nourished and protected their individualists in the motoring field until a much later date. In so doing, they harboured not one but several distinct types of sports car: it is no accident that one third of the vehicles described in this book were of French origin. The most important was the light sporting *voiturette* born in France. Sturdy, stark, draughty, noisy, and in production form inexpensive and fast in sound and fury if not always so in fact, its origins lay in the requirements of racing; in this case of the competitions for the Coupe de *L'Auto*, Coupé des Voiturettes and Grand Prix des Voiturettes, and (further south) for the Sicilian and Catalan Cups.

These races were designed initially to improve the efficiency of the small touring car, and then to encourage their development as a racing spectacle when racing for the giants declined. When the Gordon Bennett races lapsed after 1905, and the Grand Prix followed suit in 1909–11, the racing *voiturette*, and the production cars evolved from it, flourished. From about 1907, racing rules encouraged development in the search for power along the blind alley of a single cylinder of ever-increasing stroke. This was because the sciences of metallurgy and 'breathing' were in comparative infancy, and did

Fig. 2. Cottin et Desgouttes cockpit, France, 1911 (see 6)

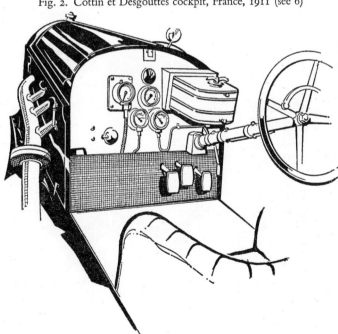

not encourage the high engine speeds possible with more cylinders. The trend is illustrated here (in modified, production form) by the Sizaire-Naudin (5). But then shorter strokes and more cylinders eventually produced not only a faster machine (since long strokes produced high piston speeds and inhibited high engine speeds) but a much more practical one for adaptation to public use. The big singles were by nature inflexible, rough, noisy, and (in extreme form) very highly stressed. The new racing cars were more flexible, smoother, easier to control; and some wholly delightful catalogued sporting cars resulted in several countries, notably the Alfonso XIII Hispano-Suiza from Spain and France (10) and the German Bugatti Type 13 (17). Lesser known vehicles such as the Grégoire from France (7) or the Italian SPA (13) were just as agreeable.

But such cars as these were not cheap. The modest man who wanted to go fast, or to seem to go fast, turned all over the motoring world first to the sporting cycle-car, such as the Morgan (30) or the GN (27). This, as its name suggested, was intended as a compromise between motor cycle and car, with all that that foreboded. Exceedingly cramped and exposed accommodation for two (or sometimes one) was

Fig. 3. Hispano-Suiza Alfonso XIII engine, Spain, c. 1911 (see 10)

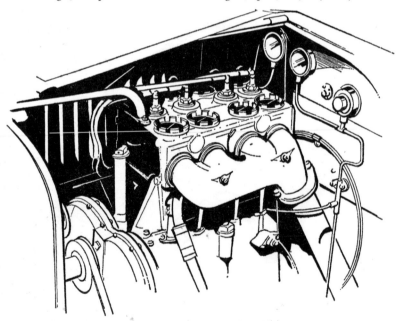

squeezed into a flimsy, vestigial frame clad in an equally insubstantial body of wood, composition or fabric. Power was provided in fair measure, if noisily and messily, by a one or two-cylinder engine of motor-cycle type, air cooled, of less than a litre's capacity, with exposed valve gear. Control was precarious at best, since the steering and brakes were usually crude and ineffective, and the belt final drive that was common tended to slip in the wet.

Cheapness, simplicity and a good power-to-weight ratio soon ceased to be enough compensation for most marginal sportsmen, who demanded something better. After the First World War the French and to some degree the Italian industry gave them what they wanted: simplicity, economy, cheapness and low weight combined with a rather more habitable if still ill-finished body suited to the tougher sort of family, and propelled by a water-cooled four-cylinder engine driving via a three-speed sliding-pinion gear-box by cardan shaft to the rear wheels—in other words a vehicle that approximated rather more than did the cycle-car to the 'proper' cars that the comfortably-off drove, even if it had no differential and the suspension was crude (by quarter-elliptic springs all round, or by a transverse half-elliptic spring at the front). Needless to say, front-wheel brakes were very late in coming, since they added weight and steering problems. These entertaining little machines were not usually called sports cars (though sports models of them were made), but they could be called so in fact, since they called for a high degree of sport-ing character in their drivers. They were quite fast, and they tended to handle well.

A few were much more than boys' racers. The Bugatti Brescia (37), the Chenard-Walcker 'Tanks' (57) and the twin o.h.c. Salmsons (60) were highly sophisticated designs that were true racing cars in miniature, carrying all before them in their classes (at Le Mans and Spa, for example, and in the Coupe Boillot at Boulogne) or in races specially organized for them, like the Bol d'Or (another 24-hour endurance test). These were not, of course, cheap cars for the masses like the rest, but they were cousins, born originally of the same needs.

The *voiturette*, in its turn, lost ground when the average Frenchman (who had held out against the trend longer than anyone else except the British) took to his Citroen, his Peugeot or his Renault *conduite intérieure tout acier*. The breed was just about extinct by the end of our period, though a few examples tottered on until about 1929. In their day, from 1920 to about 1927, they were so numerous that they constituted the typical French sporting car, from the famous Senechal (35), Salmson, Amilcar (43), BNC (42) and Benjamin (41) to the obscurities such as the Soriano-Pedroso (33), Hinstin-SUP (34), Dalila (38), Marguerite (50) and Majola (49). The breed was rare elsewhere, but its nearest foreign equivalents are exemplified here by the Swiss Speidel (84) and the British Frazer Nash (79). Incidentally, it might be claimed by the purist that some of the cars so described here were not *voiturettes* at all, but cycle-cars. According to the strict French tax-class definition

5

(by weight and cubic capacity), this is true; but in this book the terms are used loosely, to describe the two main types of light sporting car in a generally understood and accepted manner. It cannot be otherwise, since if precise definitions are to be used, the terms would mean something different from country to country.

Another important type of fast car developed initially and mainly by the Latin nations, particularly the French, was strictly a touring machine, but it was designed with the sporting Latin temperament in mind for fast long-distance motoring on Continental roads, so had many of the accepted attributes of the sports car. These fast tourers, which reached their flowering in the 1920s, were powered by efficient, if not necessarily sophisticated engines of around two litres' capacity and 50 b.h.p., sometimes with overhead valves or even an overhead camshaft, but often with side valves only. Some were purpose-designed, though others were tuned, lightened, and generally 'improved' versions of existing, solid touring cars in their maker's catalogue. Since the rakish four-passenger bodies they generally carried were light, they could be high geared, which made for high-speed cruising ability if not for lightning acceleration. Cooling and

Fig. 4. Isotta-Fraschini Tipo KM engine, Italy, c. 1912 (see 8)

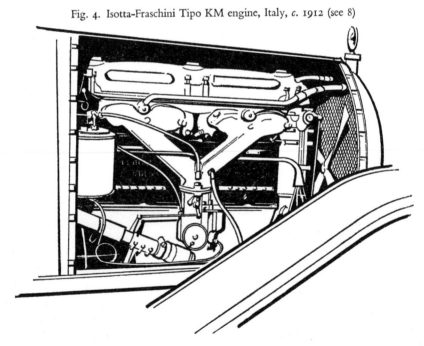

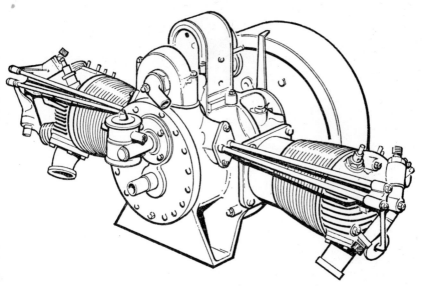

Fig. 5. ABC flat twin engine, Great Britain, *c.* 1922 (see 81)

lubrication needed to be effective, and ignition reliable. Italian examples tended to have low intermediate gears, for Alpine work. Brakes were generally good, handling qualities pleasant, and steering light (even with front wheel brakes, since many of these cars had them from the beginning—they were not afterthoughts). Examples from France were the Ballot 2LTS (56), Brasier (40), Voisin C5 (51), Bugatti Type 30 (46), and 15 CV Lorraine-Dietrich (55). Italy contributed the Ceirano Tipo CS (61), Diatto Tipo 20 (67), and Ansaldo 4CS (63). The type was common in Central Europe too, though as with other fast cars from this region, its derivation was probably ultimately from the prewar Herkomer Trials and Prince Henry Tours (*see below*). Germany offered the Fafnir Typ

471 (86), NAG C4b (88) and Stoewer D10 and D12 (87), and Austria the Austro-Daimler AD617 (91). Close relatives were the sporting derivations of luxury cars such as the Hispano-Suiza H6 (39), Isotta-Fraschini Tipo 8ASS (69), and Excelsior Albert I (96), from France, Italy and Belgium respectively. The fast tourer died from the same disease as afflicted the sporting *voiturette*: overweight, and softening of the muscles. From the middle 1920s the average buyer of medium-sized touring cars came to want six cylinders, and then eight, for flexibility and smoothness. He wanted more comfort, which meant sedan bodies, more weight, lower gearing and fussier progress. He wanted low-pressure tyres for the same reason, which led to loss of lightness and precision in handling.

7

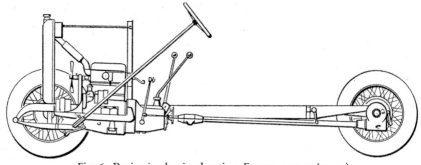

Fig. 6. Benjamin chassis, elevation, France, *c.* 1925 (see 41)

Many of these machines distinguished themselves in competitions
incidentally to their main purpose, but
in addition to the French *voiturette*
discussed earlier, there were other
classes of European sports car that arose
directly from competitions. Between
1905 and 1907 the regulations of the
German Herkomer Trials, originally
designed to foster the development of
the touring car (like the French *voiturette* races), unwittingly came to place
more and more of a premium on high
speed. The process was accelerated in
the event which succeeded the Herkomer, the Prince Henry Tours of
1908–10. When the organizers tried to
counter this tendency by limiting bore
size and imposing minimum weight
rules, manufacturers improved engine
efficiency, as in the Prince Henry-type
Benz (2) and Austro-Daimler (15).
Most of the later Prince Henry-type
cars had overhead-valve engines of
between three- and six-litre capacity,
giving up to 115 b.h.p. As the rules
controlling body dimensions grew
more lax, the competitors devised light,
wind-cheating shapes that could accom-
modate four passengers. (That
remained a stipulation.) The outcome,
first seen in (for example) the 1908
Prince Henry Horch (1), was the
origin of the sporting 'torpedo' body,
as it was called in Britain, which
(because of the success of and consequent publicity given to cars wearing
it) set the fashion for the production
models that followed the competition
cars. One offshoot of it was peculiar to
central Europe. Although it was born
purely of the need to limit frontal areas
while keeping within the regulations of
the 1909 and 1910 Prince Henry events
(*see* 1909 Prince Henry Opel [3]), the
concave-sided body was the hallmark
of the German-influenced sports car
until the middle 1920s. Ernst Neu-
mann-Nander was the most fashionable designer of such shapes. The
specialized sports car produced by the
big German events was further fostered
after they ended by the Austrian
International Alpine Tours and the
Russian Czar's Cup contests of 1910–14,
which, since there was slightly less

emphasis on speed and more on endurance, produced a less fierce breed of catalogued sports car. Between them, they prompted the appearance of the Alpine-Type Austro-Daimler (16), the Audi Alpensieger (22), the Rolls Royce Continental and Alpine Eagle (26), and the Austin Defiance (25). Naturally, the German industry, more closely concerned than any other in all these events, offered a wider variety of sporting cars than any, some of them (like the NSU, NAG and Apollo [4, 18, 21]) sports versions of touring cars, and others specialized sports machines such as the Prince Henry Austro-Daimler and the 37/90-h.p. Mercedes (19).

One of the typical British sports car types, too, was born of competitions. The Rolls-Royce London-Edinburgh (23), the Talbot Competition (28), and (in spite of its name) the Prince Henry Vauxhall (24) had their origins in three very British forms of contest —the long-distance road trials of the 1905-9 period (notably the 2000 Miles Trial of 1908), the Tourist Trophy races of 1905-7, and the pure racing made possible by the existence of Brooklands Motor Course from 1907. The latter was Britain's first purpose-built racing track. In the first two types of competition, machines that were, and remained, strictly practical touring cars were developed to a greater degree of mechanical efficiency. That is, their power-to-cubic-capacity ratio was improved. Lighter reciprocating parts, better breathing, improved combustion chamber design and higher compression ratios produced higher engine speeds and thus more power from given engine sizes. Brooklands Motor Course allowed much greater scope for development of the same type of vehicle, since very high sustained speed was now possible for

Fig. 7. Darmont chassis frame, France, c. 1925

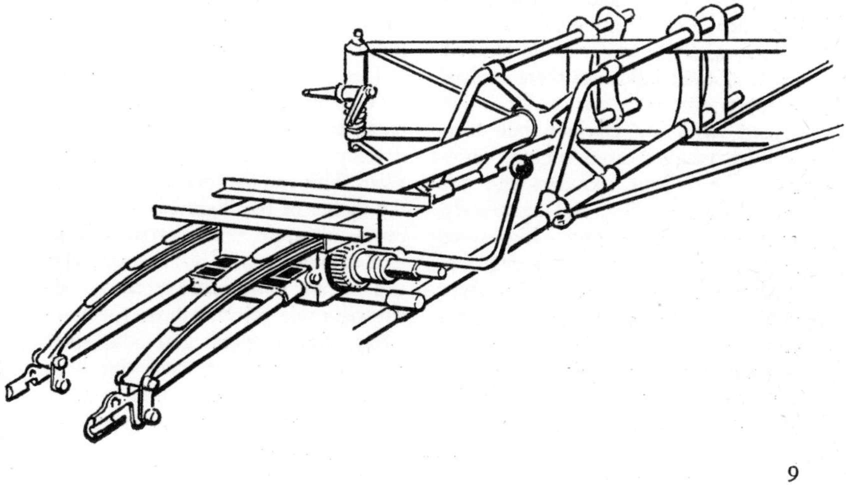

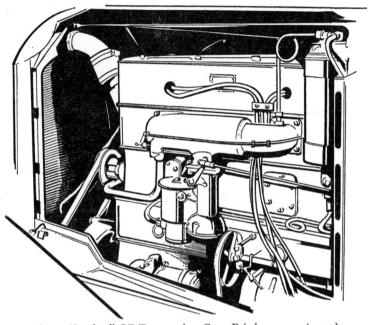

Fig. 8. Vauxhaull OE-Type engine, Great Britain, *c.* 1924 (see 73)

the first in Britain. Aerodynamic efficiency became important at such velocities, and was closely studied. From all these influences there evolved a sports car that was really a fast tourer, with its efficient but low-stressed, medium-sized engine, customarily with four cylinders and side valves, high gearing, and light body, combining mile-eating high-speed reliability with (usually) a fair degree of comfort and high quality. The type persisted into the middle 1920s, exemplified by the Vauxhall 30/98 (73), successor to the Prince Henry Vauxhall, the Austin Brooklands Sports Model (72) and, in miniature, by the Aston

Martin (75). It was killed by the same factors that put paid to the French and Italian fast tourer (*see above*).

The other typically British sports-car type began to evolve (from the same roots) before 1914, and reached its full development in the early and middle 1920s. This was the sporting variant on the theme of the 'light car'—the big-car-in-miniature, with its water-cooled four-cylinder engine of between one and one and a half litre's capacity, usually with side valves, a three- (or more rarely, four-) speed gear-box, shaft drive to a live rear axle, and half-elliptic suspension all round. It grew up in every major car-producing country of Europe from around 1912 on, eventually (thanks to its 'big-car' comfort, flexibility and smoothness) supplanting the cycle-car and (in France) even the little *voiturette* described, which was an altogether less substantial proposition. However, only in Britain did the sports version of this family light car really catch on. There, almost every manufacturer who offered a light car in the 1920s catalogued a sports model, with a lighter, more attractive body, higher gearing, and (usually) a mildly tuned engine in which reliability was not sacrificed to speed. Top speed would be around 60 m.p.h., instead of the 40–50 m.p.h. of its more solid, stodgy parent. Its main advantage was that, in the case of mass-produced makes, the sports car benefited from the widespread spares and servicing facilities afforded to the family car. Examples of this type shown here are the Calthorpe (70), Morris (71), MG (78), Riley (76) and Bayliss-Thomas (80). A few machines in the light-car class were pretty sporting in their strictly touring form, so their true sports versions were considerably more exciting—such were the Alvis 12/50 (77) and the ABC (81). Close foreign equivalents were rare. France, which had its own special breed of small sports car, had the Talbot (52), Italy could show the Fiat 501S (64), Chiribiri (65) and Ceirano (66), Germany the NSU 5/30 PS (90), and Czechoslovakia its Tatra (93). In Britain, the type died when around 1928, a new breed of smaller, cheaper, lighter (though lower-geared), more efficient family car replaced the old, and its own sports alternatives duly appeared—derivations of the Morris

Minor (in the form of the M-type MG), the Singer Junior, the Riley Nine, the Standard Nine, and so on.

The typical sports car of the period under consideration in this book reached its high point in the early and middle 1920s. In its most exciting and fastest form, it was still a biggish car of anything between two and five (or even more) litres' capacity—the miniature breeds were still to supplant it. It did not fit exactly into any of the categories discussed, because it was the product, the culmination in one splendid machine, of several of the influences noted as well as of others—the accelerating influence of pure racing-car design, and of First World War aero-engine experience. The latter in particular had encouraged the widespread use of light alloys for weight-saving, better heat dissipation, and higher revolutions, and had facilitated great advances in reliability at long-sustained high speeds and extreme stresses. Much was learned about efficient lubrication, cooling and ignition under such conditions, and about the extraction of maximum power from engines of relatively low weight and small size. The machine was hammered into its final shape by the new races designed to foster the sports car that were introduced early in the decade: the Le Mans 24-hour races, the Belgian Grand Prix at Spa, the Coppa Florio, the contest for the Coupe Boillot at Boulogne, and their like. It is illustrated here by the Three-Litre Bentley and Super-Sports Sunbeam from Britain (82, 83), the Bignan and Ballot 2LS from France (36, 45), the SPA and Alfa Romeo RLSS from Italy (62, 68), the German Mercedes

28/95PS and Steiger (85, 89), the Austrian Steyr (92), and the Belgian Métallurgique and Imperia (94, 95). Almost all had one or two overhead camshafts, four valves per cylinder were not unusual, engine speeds of 3500–4000 r.p.m. or more were common, and 25–30 b.h.p. per litre was normal. The ruling sports car of 1925 had caught up with the Grand Prix car of 1914 or even 1919. It was only to be displaced from its eminence when manufactures such as Alfa Romeo introduced a type that had all these advantages coupled with those afforded by lower weight, a lower centre of gravity, and more compactness.

It is easy to be carried away by the glamour of such machines into thinking that they were more numerous and significant than was actually the case, in the context of motoring as a whole.

Then, as now, the type was a pure luxury. Its importance to the world's motor industry was negligible, except in so far as its adventures in competition and aura of romance boosted the sales of its hack stablemates, and helped to test and develop innovation in design. The RLSS Alfa Romeo, sold a total of 329 units in three years; and the Three Litre Bentley, costing £1125 ($5625) in 1924–5, 1600 in nine years. In contrast, at least 45,000 of the humble Fiat 501 were made in seven seasons, while no fewer than 61,000-odd Morrises were made in 1927 alone, when the price of a basic two-passenger Cowley was £148 10s. ($742). The sound and fury of the finest sports cars of the middle 1920s might have been splendid and awe-inspiring, but it was encountered more rarely than its reputation then and now suggests.

AUTHOR'S NOTES

The dates given to the cars painted are usually of the particular vehicles illustrated, or, if the precise date is unknown, of the currency of the model. A reference to the descriptive text under 'The Sports Cars in Detail' (pp. 109-161) will tell the reader which applies.

The colouring of a car as shown is not necessarily that in which it was normally seen or catalogued. It has been dictated by the exigencies of an attractive page layout. In many instances, though, cars were to be seen, if not catalogued, in almost any colour, since this could be at the discretion of the buyer (particularly in the cases of custom built bodies).

For the sake of interest and to provide an idea of the variety to be seen on the basic model, different body styles, etc. are illustrated, even if unusual, i.e. they are not necessarily representative.

Any two views of one car are not necessarily to scale; nor are the views of different cars on the same or adjoining pages.

Approximate conversion of cylinder bore and stroke: 25·4 millimetres (mm.) = 1 inch.

Approximate conversion of engine cubic capacity: 16·4 cubic centimetres (c.c.) = 1 cubic inch.

1

Horch 18/22 PS, 1908. Germany. Water cooled, four vertical cylinders in line. 85 × 120 mm., 2725 cc. Overhead inlet valves, side exhaust valves. Four forward speeds. Half-elliptic springs front and rear. Shaft drive.

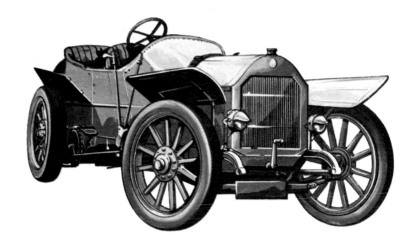

2

Benz, Prince Henry type, 1908, 1910. Germany. Water cooled, four vertical cylinders in line. *Top:* 115 × 160 mm. or 180 mm., 6658 or 7481 cc. Two valves per cylinder. Pushrod-operated overhead valves. Chain drive. *Bottom:* 115 × 175 mm., 7271 cc. Four valves per cylinder. Pushrod-operated overhead valves. Shaft drive. Four forward speeds. Half-elliptic springs front and rear.

3

Opel 8 PS, 1909. Germany. Water cooled, four vertical cylinders in line. 70 × 125 mm., 1925 cc. Side valves in L head. Four forward speeds. Half-elliptic springs front and rear. Shaft drive.

4

NSU 10/30 PS, 1912; 10/28 PS, 1909. Germany. Water cooled, four vertical
cylinders in line. 85 × 115 mm., 2608 cc. *Top:* Overhead inlet valves, side
exhaust valves; *bottom:* side valves in T head. Four forward speeds. Half-
elliptic springs front and rear. Shaft drive.

5

Sizaire-Naudin, 1908. France. Water cooled, single vertical cylinder. Bore 120 mm., various strokes. Overhead inlet valve, side exhaust valve. Three forward speeds. Independent front suspension by sliding pillars and transverse leaf spring, quarter-elliptic springs at rear. Shaft drive.

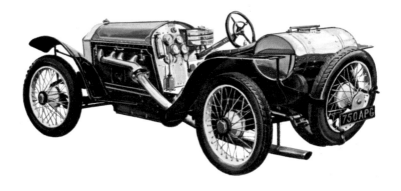

6

Cottin et Desgouttes, 1911. France. Water cooled, four cylinders in line. 120 × 160 mm., 7241 cc. Side valves in T head. Four forward speeds. Half-elliptic springs front and rear. Chain drive.

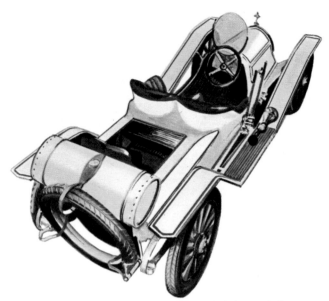

7

Grégoire 13/18CV, 1911; 14/24CV, 1913. France. Water cooled, four vertical cylinders in line. *Top:* 80 × 110 mm., 2212 cc.; *bottom:* 80 × 160 mm., 3217 cc. Side valves in L head. *Top:* three forward speeds; *bottom:* four forward speeds. Half-elliptic springs front and rear. Shaft drive.

8

Isotta-Fraschini Tipo KM, 1912, 1914. Italy. Water cooled, four vertical cylinders in line. 130 × 200 mm., 10,623 cc. Four overhead valves per cylinder, actuated by single overhead camshaft. Four forward speeds. Front wheel brakes. Half-elliptic springs front and rear. Chain drive.

9

SPA, 1913. Italy. Water cooled, four vertical cylinders in line. 100 × 140 mm., 4400 cc. Side valves. Four forward speeds. Half-elliptic springs front and rear. Shaft drive.

HISPANO-SUIZA ALFONSO XIII

10

Hispano-Suiza Alfonso XIII, 1914, 1911. Spain, France. Water cooled, four vertical cylinders in line. 80 × 180 mm., 3624 cc. Side valves in T head. Three or four forward speeds. Half-elliptic springs at front, half-elliptic or three-quarter elliptic springs at rear. Shaft drive.

11

Stanley Gentleman's Speedy Roadster, 1907, 1908. USA. Steam engine, simple, double acting. Two horizontal cylinders. Vertical multi-tube boiler, kerosene burner. Full-elliptic springs front and rear.

LOZIER 50 H.P.

12

Lozier 50 h.p., 1913, 1910. USA. Water cooled, six vertical cylinders in line. 117·5 × 140 mm., 9112 cc. Side valves in T head. Four forward speeds. Half-elliptic springs front and rear. Shaft drive.

13

Mercer Type 35R, 1911; 35J, 1913. USA. Water cooled, four vertical cylinders in line. 111 × 127 mm., 4940 cc. Side valves in T head. Three or four forward speeds. Half-elliptic springs front and rear. Shaft drive.

STUTZ BEARCAT

14

Stutz Bearcat, 1914, 1921. USA. Water cooled, four vertical cylinders in line. 121 × 140 mm., 6396 cc. Side valves in T head. Three forward speeds. Half-elliptic springs front and rear. Shaft drive.

15

Austro-Daimler Prince Henry, 1914. Austria. Water cooled, four vertical cylinders in line. 105 x 165-mm., 5714 cc. Five overhead valves per cylinder, actuated by single overhead camshaft. Four forward speeds. Half-elliptic springs front and rear. Shaft drive.

AUSTRO-DAIMLER ALPENTYP

16

Austro-Daimler Alpentyp, 1912. Austria. Water cooled, four vertical cylinders in line. 80 × 110 mm., 2212 cc. Side valves in L head. Four forward speeds. Half-elliptic springs front and rear. Shaft drive.

17

Bugatti Type 13, 1910, 1914. Germany. Water cooled, four vertical cylinders
in line. 65 × 100 mm., 1327 cc. Two valves per cylinder, actuated by single
overhead camshaft. Four forward speeds. *Top:* Half-elliptic front springs, at
rear double half-elliptic springs; *bottom:* reversed quarter-elliptic springs at
rear. Shaft drive.

18

NAG Typ K5, 1912, 1914. Germany. Water cooled, four vertical cylinders in line. 90 × 130 mm., 3370 cc. Side valves in L head. Four forward speeds. Half-elliptic front springs, three-quarter elliptic rear springs. Shaft drive.

19

Mercedes 37/90 PS, 16/45 PS, 1913. Germany. Water cooled, four vertical cylinders in line. *Top*: 130 × 180 mm., 9500 cc. Three pushrod-operated overhead valves per cylinder (one inlet, two exhaust). Four forward speeds. Half-elliptic springs front and rear. Chain drive. *Bottom*: 100 × 130 mm., 4084 cc. Knight sleeve valves. Four forward speeds. Half-elliptic springs front and rear. Shaft drive.

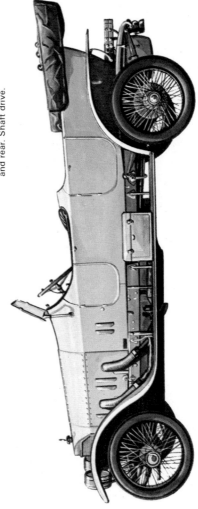

20

Bugatti, 1913. Germany. Water cooled, four vertical cylinders in line. 100 × 160 mm., 5027 cc. Three valves per cylinder actuated by single overhead camshaft. Four forward speeds. Double half-elliptic front springs, reversed quarter-elliptic rear springs. Chain drive.

21

Apollo Typ F Rekord, 1913. Germany. Water cooled, four vertical cylinders in line. 75 × 116 mm., 2040 cc. Pushrod-operated overhead valves. Four forward speeds. Half-elliptic springs front and rear. Shaft drive.

AUDI ALPENSIEGER

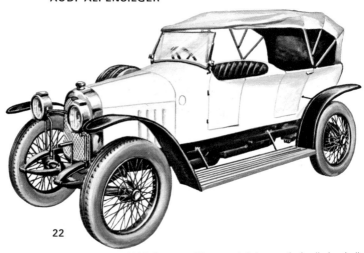

22

Audi Alpensieger, 1914. Germany. Water cooled, four vertical cylinders in line. 90 × 140 mm., 3564 cc. Overhead inlet valves, side exhaust valves. Four forward speeds. Half-elliptic springs front and rear. Shaft drive.

23

Rolls Royce London-Edinburgh, 1911, 1913. Great Britain. Water cooled, six vertical cylinders in line. 114 × 121 mm., 7410 cc. Side valves in L head. *Top:* three forward speeds; *bottom:* four forward speeds. Half-elliptic front springs, cantilever rear springs. Shaft drive.

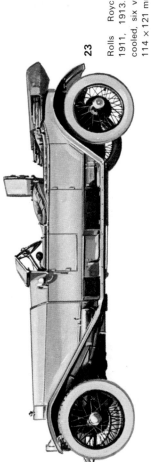

VAUXHALL PRINCE HENRY

24

Vauxhall Prince Henry, 1913, 1912. Great Britain. Water cooled, four vertical cylinders in line. *Top:* 95 × 140 mm., 3971 cc.; *bottom:* 90 × 120 mm., 3055 cc. Side valves in L head. Four forward speeds. Half-elliptic springs front and rear. Shaft drive.

25

Austin Defiance, 1912. Great Britain. Water cooled, four vertical cylinders in
line. 126 × 127 mm., 6329 cc. Side valves in T head. Four forward speeds.
Half-elliptic springs front and rear. Shaft drive.

26

Rolls Royce Continental, 1913: Alpine Eagle, 1914. Great Britain. Water cooled, six vertical cylinders in line. 114 x 121 mm., 7410 cc. Side valves in L head. Four forward speeds. Half-elliptic front springs, cantilever rear springs. Shaft drive.

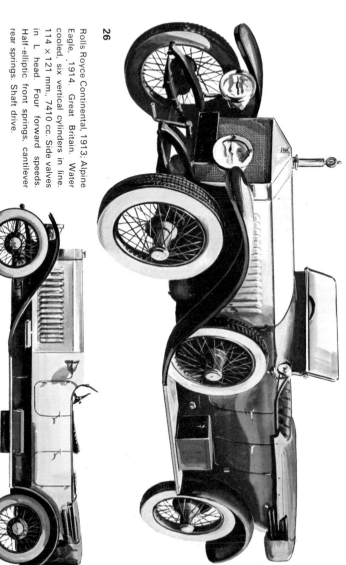

27

GN, 1920, 1913. Great Britain. Air cooled, two cylinders in vee formation.
84 × 98 mm., 1086 cc. Overhead inlet valves, side exhaust valves. *Top:* three
forward speeds, chain final drive; *bottom:* two forward speeds, belt final
drive. Quarter-elliptic springs front and rear.

TALBOT COMPETITION

28

Talbot Competition, 1914. Great Britain. Water cooled, four vertical cylinders in line. 101 × 140 mm., 4447 cc. Side valves in L head. Four forward speeds. Half-elliptic springs front and rear. Shaft drive.

29

Lanchester Sporting Forty, 1914. Great Britain. Water cooled, six vertical cylinders in line. 101·6 × 114·3 mm., 5588 cc. Side valves in L head. Three forward speeds. Front half-elliptic springs, rear cantilever springs. Shaft drive.

30

Morgan Grand Prix, 1915. Great Britain. Water cooled, two cylinders in vee formation. 90 × 77·5 mm., 986 cc. Side or pushrod-operated overhead valves. Two forward speeds. Independent front suspension by sliding pillars and coil springs. Chain drive.

31

Cunningham, 1919–20. U.S.A. Water cooled, eight cylinders in vee formation. 95 × 127 mm., 7204 cc. Side valves in L head. Four·forward speeds.
Front half-elliptic springs, rear three-quarter elliptic springs. Shaft drive.

KISSEL 6-55, 8-75

32

Kissel 6-55, 1924; 8-75, 1927. U.S.A. Water cooled. *Top:* 84 x 130 mm., 4671 cc.; eight vertical cylinders in line; *bottom:* 81 x 114 mm., 4712 cc. Six cylinders. Side valves in L head. Three forward speeds. Half-elliptic springs front and rear. Shaft drive.

33

Soriano-Pedroso 6/8 CV, 1920. France. Water cooled, four vertical cylinders in line. 60 × 100 mm., 1130 cc. Side valves in L head. Three forward speeds. Front half-elliptic springs, rear cantilever springs. Chain final drive.

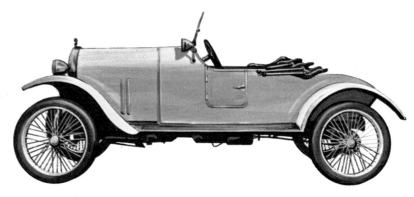

34

Hinstin S.U.P., 1921. France. Water cooled, four vertical cylinders in line. 62 × 91 mm., 1100 cc. Pushrod-operated overhead valves. Three forward speeds. Single transverse spring at front, quarter-elliptic springs at rear. Shaft drive.

35

Sénéchal, 1921, 1925. France. Water cooled, 4 vertical cylinders in line. *Top:* 55 × 95 mm., 5903 cc.; *bottom:* 59 × 100 mm., 1094 cc. *Top:* Side valves in L head, two forward speeds; *bottom:* Pushrod-operated overhead valves, three forward speeds. Single transverse spring at front, quarter-elliptic springs at rear. Shaft drive.

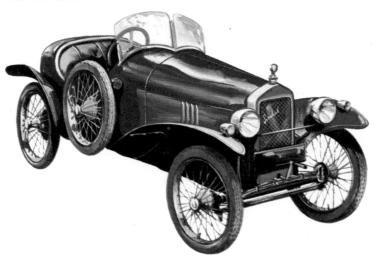

36

Bignan, 1922. France. Water cooled, four vertical cylinders in line. 75 × 112 mm., 1980 cc. Desmodromic (positively closed) valves. Four forward speeds. Half-elliptic springs front and rear. Shaft drive.

37

Bugatti Brescia Type 23, 1922. France. Water cooled, four vertical cylinders in line. 69 × 100 mm., 1496 cc. Four valves per cylinder, actuated by single overhead camshaft. Four forward speeds. Front half-elliptic front springs, rear reversed quarter-elliptic springs. Shaft drive.

DALILA

38

Dalila, 1922. France. Water cooled, four vertical cylinders in line. 57 × 95 mm., 962 cc. Side valves in L head. Three forward speeds. Independent four-wheel suspension by articulated levers and quarter-elliptic springs. Shaft drive.

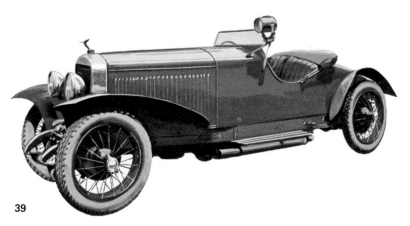

39

Hispano-Suiza H6, 1922; H6C, 1926. France. Water cooled, six vertical cylinders in line. *Top:* 100 × 140 mm., 6600 cc.; *bottom:* 110 × 140 mm., 7986 cc. Overhead valves actuated by single overhead camshaft. Three forward speeds. Half-elliptic springs front and rear. Shaft drive.

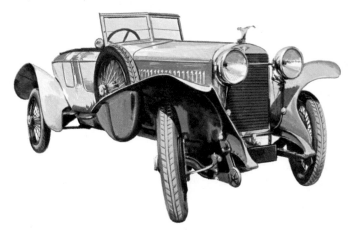

40

Brasier TC4, 1923, 1924. France. Water cooled, four vertical cylinders in line. 74 × 120 mm., 2094 cc. Pushrod-operated overhead valves. Four forward speeds. Half-elliptic springs front and rear. Shaft drive.

41

Benjamin P2, 1923; Bol d'Or type, 1925. France. Water cooled, four vertical cylinders in line. *Top:* two-cylinder two-stroke, 66 × 80 mm., 548 cc.; *bottom:* 54 × 82 mm., 750 cc. Side valves in L head. Three forward speeds. Single transverse spring at front, quarter-elliptic springs at rear. Shaft drive.

BNC

42

BNC, 1923. France. Water cooled, four vertical cylinders in line. 55 × 94 mm., 892 cc. Side valves in L head. Three forward speeds. Front half-elliptic springs, rear cantilever springs. Shaft drive.

43

Amilcar Type CC, 1923. France. Water cooled, four vertical cylinders in line. 55 × 95 mm., 903 cc. Side valves in L head. Three forward speeds. Quarter-elliptic springs front and rear. Shaft drive.

44

Sandford, 1924–25. France. Water cooled, four vertical cylinders in line. 59 × 100 mm., 1095 cc. Pushrod-operated overhead valves. Three forward speeds. Independent front suspension by sliding pillars and coil springs. Chain final drive.

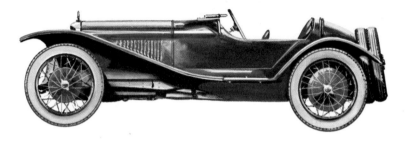

45

Ballot 2LS, 1924. France. Water cooled, four vertical cylinders in line. 70 × 130 mm., 1995 cc. Four overhead valves per cylinder actuated by two overhead camshafts. Four forward speeds. Half-elliptic springs front and rear. Shaft drive.

46

Bugatti Type 30, 1924, 1925. France. Water cooled, eight vertical cylinders in line. 60 × 88 mm., 1991 cc. Three overhead valves per cylinder, actuated by single overhead camshaft. Four forward speeds. Front half-elliptic springs, rear reversed quarter-elliptic springs. Shaft drive.

Chenard-Walcker Type X, 1924, 1925. France. Water cooled, eight vertical cylinders in line. 69·5 × 130 mm., 3904 cc. Overhead valves actuated by single overhead camshaft. Four forward speeds. Half-elliptic springs front and rear. Shaft drive.

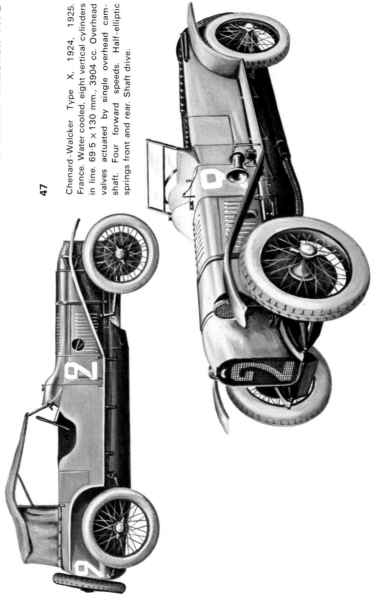

D'YRSAN

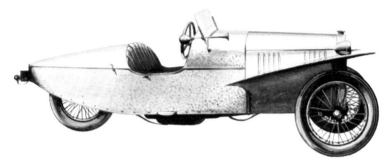

48

D'Yrsan, 1924, 1927. France. Water cooled, four vertical cylinders in line. 57 × 95 mm., 972 cc. Pushrod-operated overhead valves. Three forward speeds. Independent front suspension by two superimposed transverse springs, rear suspension by two quarter-elliptic springs. Shaft primary drive, chain final drive.

49

Majola Type DT, 1925. France. Water cooled, four vertical cylinders in line. 65 × 105 mm., 1390 cc. Overhead valves actuated by single overhead camshaft. Four forward speeds. Half-elliptic springs front and rear. Shaft drive.

MARGUERITE TYPE B0

50

Marguerite Type B0, 1925. France. Water cooled, four vertical cylinders in line. 59 × 100 mm., 1094 cc. Pushrod-operated overhead valves. Three forward speeds. Half-elliptic springs front and rear. Shaft drive.

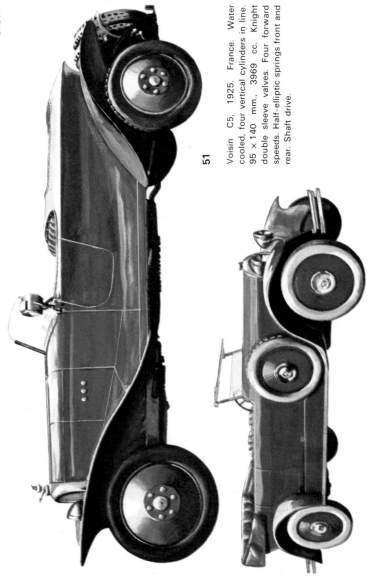

51

Voisin C5, 1925. France. Water cooled, four vertical cylinders in line. 95 × 140 mm., 3969 cc. Knight double sleeve valves. Four forward speeds. Half-elliptic springs front and rear. Shaft drive.

TALBOT TYPE 2SC DC

52

Talbot Type 2SC, DC, 1925. France. Water cooled, four vertical cylinders in line. *Top:* 68 × 103 mm., 1496 cc.; *bottom:* 68 × 110 mm., 1598 cc. Pushrod-operated overhead valves. Three forward speeds. Front half-elliptic springs, rear cantilever springs. Shaft drive.

53

GM, 1925. France. Water cooled, four vertical cylinders in line. 68 × 103 mm.,
1496 cc. Overhead valves actuated by single overhead camshaft. Four forward
speeds. Half-elliptic springs front and rear. Shaft drive.

EHP

54

EHP, 1925–26. France. Water cooled, four vertical cylinders in line. 68 × 103 mm., 1496 cc. Overhead valves actuated by single overhead camshaft. Four forward speeds. Front half-elliptic springs, rear quarter-elliptic springs. Shaft drive.

55

Lorraine-Dietrich 15CV Sport, 1925, 1926. France. Water cooled, six vertical cylinders in line. 75 × 130 mm., 3446 cc. Pushrod-operated overhead valves. Three forward speeds. Front half-elliptic springs, rear cantilever springs. Shaft drive.

BALLOT 2LTS

56

Ballot 2LTS, 1926. France. Water cooled, four vertical cylinders in line. 70 × 130 mm., 1995 cc. Overhead valves actuated by single overhead camshaft. Four forward speeds. Half-elliptic springs front and rear. Shaft drive.

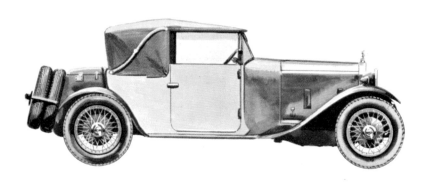

57

Chenard-Walcker, 1926. France. Water cooled, four vertical cylinders in line. 66 × 80 mm., 1095 cc. Pushrod-operated overhead valves. Four forward speeds. Half-elliptic springs front and rear. Shaft drive.

RATIER

58

Ratier, 1926. France. Water cooled, four vertical cylinders in line. 60 × 66 mm., 746 cc. Overhead valves actuated by single overhead camshaft. Three forward speeds. Front half-elliptic springs, rear reversed quarter-elliptic springs. Shaft drive.

59

SCAP 6CV, 1926, 1927. France. Water cooled, four vertical cylinders in line. 63 × 87 mm., 1085 cc. Pushrod-operated overhead valves. Four forward speeds. Half-elliptic springs front and rear. Shaft drive.

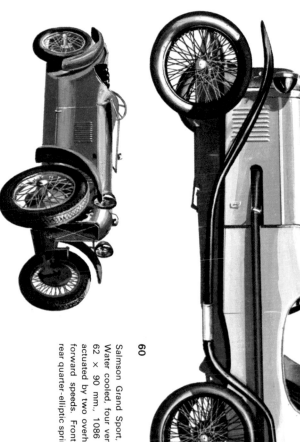

60

Salmson Grand Sport, 1926, 1927. France. Water cooled, four vertical cylinders in line. 62 × 90 mm., 1086 cc. Overhead valves actuated by two overhead camshafts. Three forward speeds. Front half-elliptic springs, rear quarter-elliptic springs. Shaft drive.

61

Ceirano Tipo CS, 1921. Italy. Water cooled, four vertical cylinders in line. 75 × 130 mm., 2166 cc. Side valves in L head. Four forward speeds. Half-elliptic springs front and rear. Shaft drive.

62

SPA, 1921, 1922. Italy. Water cooled, six vertical cylinders in line. 85 × 130 mm., 4420 cc. Overhead valves actuated by two overhead camshafts. Four forward speeds. Front half-elliptic springs, rear cantilever springs. Shaft drive.

63

Ansaldo Tipo 4CS, 1923. Italy. Water cooled, four vertical cylinders in line. 72·5 × 120 mm., 1981 cc. Overhead valves actuated by single overhead camshaft. Three forward speeds. Half-elliptic springs front and rear. Shaft drive.

64

Fiat Tipo 501S, 1924. Italy. Water cooled, four vertical cylinders in line. 65 × 110 mm., 1460 cc. Side valves in L head. Four forward speeds. Half-elliptic springs front and rear. Shaft drive.

65

Chiribiri Milano, Monza Normale, 1925. Italy. Water cooled, four vertical cylinders in line. *Top:* 65 × 112 mm., 1485 cc. Side valves in L head; *bottom:* overhead valves actuated by single overhead camshaft. Four forward speeds. Half-elliptic springs front and rear. Shaft drive.

CEIRANO TIPO N150S, N150

66

Ceirano Tipo N150S, N150, 1925. Italy. Water cooled, four vertical cylinders in line. 65 × 110 mm., 1460 cc. *Top:* Pushrod-operated overhead valves; *bottom:* side valves in L head. Four forward speeds. Half-elliptic springs front and rear. Shaft drive.

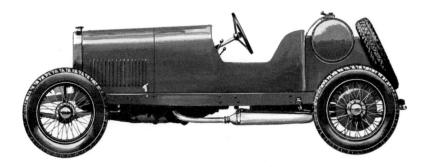

67

Diatto Tipo 20, 1925. Italy. Water cooled, four vertical cylinders in line. 80 × 100 mm., 1996 cc. Overhead valves actuated by single overhead cam-shaft. Four forward speeds. Front half-elliptic springs, rear cantilever springs. Shaft drive.

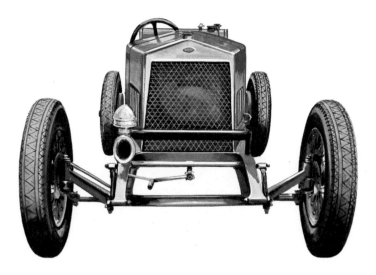

ALFA ROMEO RLSS

68

Alfa Romeo RLSS, 1925, 1927. Italy. Water cooled, six vertical cylinders in line. 76 × 110 mm., 2994 cc. Pushrod-operated overhead valves. Four forward speeds. Half-elliptic springs front and rear. Shaft drive.

ISOTTA-FRASCHINI TIPO 8ASS

69

Isotta-Fraschini Tipo 8ASS, 1926. Italy. Water cooled, eight vertical cylinders in line. 95 × 130 mm., 7370 cc. Pushrod-operated overhead valves. Three forward speeds. Half-elliptic springs front and rear. Shaft drive.

CALTHORPE SPORTING FOUR, SUPER SPORTS

70

Calthorpe Sporting Four, Super Sports, 1920. Great Britain. Water cooled, four vertical cylinders in line. 65 × 95 mm., 1260 cc. Side valves in L head. Three forward speeds. Half-elliptic springs front and rear. Shaft drive.

71

Morris Sports Cowley, 1921. Great Britain. Water cooled, four vertical cylinders
in line. 69·5 × 102 mm., 1548 cc. Side valves in L head. Three forward speeds.
Front half-elliptic springs, rear three-quarter elliptic springs. Shaft drive.

AUSTIN BROOKLANDS SPORTS MODEL

72

Austin Brooklands Sports Model, 1921. Great Britain. Water cooled, four vertical cylinders in line. 95 × 127 mm., 3610 cc. Side valves in L head. Four forward speeds. Half-elliptic springs front and rear. Shaft drive.

73

Vauxhall OE-Type, 1924; E-Type, 1922. Great Britain. Water cooled, four vertical cylinders in line. *Top:* 98 × 140 mm., 4224 cc.; pushrod-operated overhead valves; *bottom:* 98 × 150 mm., 4525 cc., side valves in L head. Four forward speeds. Half-elliptic springs front and rear. Shaft drive.

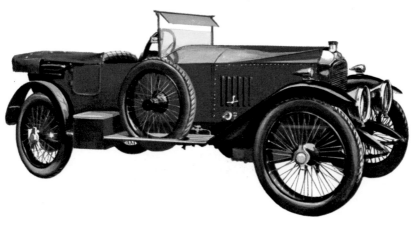

STRAKER-SQUIRE SIX

74

Straker-Squire Six, 1922, 1925. Great Britain. Water cooled, six vertical cylinders in line. 80 x 130 mm., 3900 cc. Overhead valves actuated by single overhead camshaft. Four forward speeds. Front half-elliptic springs, rear cantilever springs. Shaft drive.

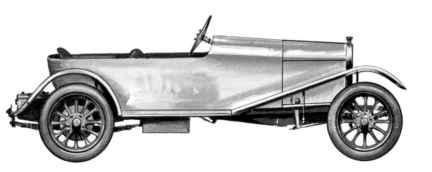

75

Aston Martin, 1923. Great Britain. Water cooled, four vertical cylinders in line. 66·5 × 107 mm., 1486 cc. Side valves in L head. Four forward speeds. Half-elliptic springs front and rear. Shaft drive.

RILEY

76

Riley, 1924. Great Britain. Water cooled, four vertical cylinders in line. 66 × 110 mm., 1498 cc. Side valves in L head. Four forward speeds. Half-elliptic springs front and rear. Shaft drive.

77

Alvis 12/50 Super Sports, 1924. Great Britain. Water cooled, four vertical cylinders in line. 68 × 103 mm., 1496 cc. Pushrod-operated overhead valves. Four forward speeds. Half-elliptic springs front and rear. Shaft drive.

78

MG Super Sports, 1925. Great Britain. Water cooled, four vertical cylinders
in line. 75 × 102 mm., 1802 cc. Side valves in L head. Three forward speeds.
Half-elliptic springs front and rear. Shaft drive.

79

Frazer Nash Fast Tourer, 1925. Great Britain. Water cooled, four vertical cylinders in line. 69 × 100 mm., 1496 cc. Side valves in L head. Three forward speeds. Quarter-elliptic springs front and rear. Chain drive.

BAYLISS-THOMAS 10/20 H.P.

80

Bayliss-Thomas 10/20 h.p., 1924. Great Britain. Water cooled, four vertical cylinders in line. 63 × 100 mm., 1247 cc. Side valves in L head. Three forward speeds. Half-elliptic springs front and rear. Shaft drive.

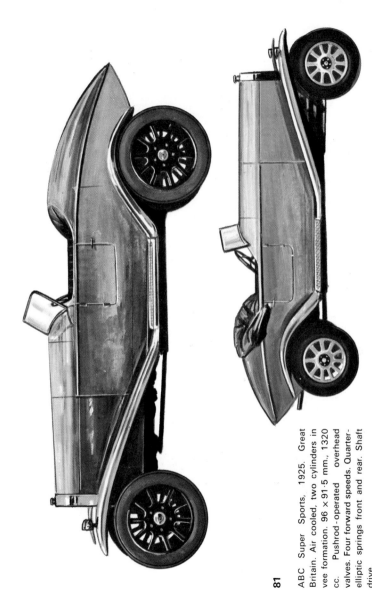

81

ABC Super Sports, 1925. Great Britain. Air cooled, two cylinders in vee formation. 96 × 91·5 mm., 1320 cc. Pushrod - operated overhead valves. Four forward speeds. Quarter - elliptic springs front and rear. Shaft drive.

BENTLEY SUPER SPORTS, SPEED MODEL

82

Bentley Super Sports, Speed Model, 1926. Great Britain. Water cooled, four vertical cylinders in line. 80 × 149 mm., 2996 cc. Overhead valves actuated by single overhead camshaft. Four forward speeds. Half-elliptic springs front and rear. Shaft drive.

83

Sunbeam Three Litre Super Sports, 1926. Great Britain. Water cooled, six vertical cylinders in line. 75 × 110 mm., 2916 cc. Overhead valves actuated by two overhead camshafts. Four forward speeds. Front half-elliptic springs, rear cantilever springs. Shaft drive.

84

Speidel 8CV, 1919, 1920. Switzerland. Water cooled, four vertical cylinders in line. 64 × 85 mm., 1094 cc. *Top:* three forward speeds; *bottom:* four forward speeds. Shaft drive. Front quarter-elliptic springs, rear half-elliptic springs.

85

Mercedes 28/95 PS, 1922, 1924. Germany.
Water cooled, six vertical cylinders in line.
105 × 140 mm., 7250 cc. Overhead valves
actuated by single overhead camshaft. Four
forward speeds. Half-elliptic springs front
and rear. Shaft drive.

86

Fafnir Typ 471, 1923. Germany. Water cooled, four vertical cylinders in line. 71 × 125 mm., 1950 cc. Pushrod-operated overhead valves. Four forward speeds. Half-elliptic springs front and rear. Shaft drive.

87

Stoewer D10, D12, 1924. Germany. Water cooled. *Top:* four vertical cylinders
in line, 83 × 120 mm., 2580 cc.; *bottom:* six cylinders, 75 × 118 mm., 3107 cc.
Side valves in L head. Four forward speeds. Half-elliptic springs front and
rear. Shaft drive.

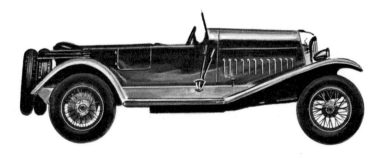

88

NAG C4b, 1924. Germany. Water cooled, four vertical cylinders in line. 83 × 118 mm., 2536 cc. Side valves in L head. Four forward speeds. Half-elliptic springs front and rear. Shaft drive.

89

Steiger Sport, 1924. Germany. Water cooled, four vertical cylinders in line. 76 × 160 mm., 2904 cc. Overhead valves actuated by single overhead camshaft. Four forward speeds. Front half-elliptic springs, rear cantilever springs (to 1924); rear half-elliptic springs (from 1924). Shaft drive.

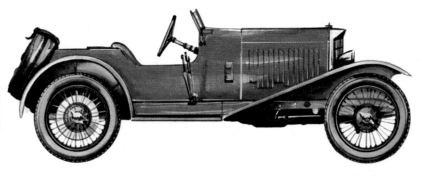

90

NSU 5/15 PS, 5/30 PS Sport, 1925. Germany. Water cooled, four vertical cylinders in line. 68 × 90 mm., 1300 cc. Side valves in L head. Four forward speeds. Half-elliptic springs front and rear. Shaft drive.

Austro-Daimler AD617, 1921; ADV, 1923. Austria. Water cooled, six vertical cylinders in line. 85 × 130 mm., 4420 cc. Overhead valves actuated by single overhead camshaft. Four forward speeds. Front half-elliptic springs, rear cantilever springs. Shaft drive.

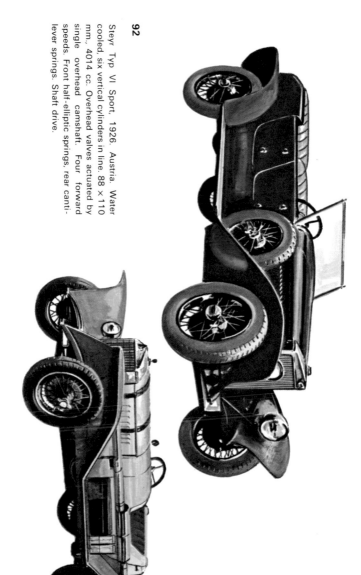

92

Steyr Typ VI Sport, 1926. Austria. Water cooled, six vertical cylinders in line. 88 × 110 mm., 4014 cc. Overhead valves actuated by single overhead camshaft. Four forward speeds. Front half-elliptic springs, rear canti-lever springs. Shaft drive.

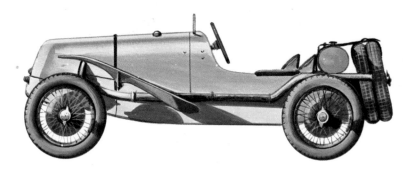

93

Tatra Typ 11, 1925. Czechoslovakia. Air cooled, two horizontally-opposed cylinders. 82 × 100 mm., 1050 cc. Pushrod-operated overhead valves. Four forward speeds. Swing axle and transverse leaf spring suspension front and rear (Targa Florio type illustrated).

MÉTALLURGIQUE

94

Métallurgique, 1922. Belgium. Water cooled, four vertical cylinders in line. 80 × 148 mm., 2974 cc. Four overhead valves per cylinder actuated by single overhead camshaft. Four forward speeds. Half-elliptic springs front and rear. Shaft drive.

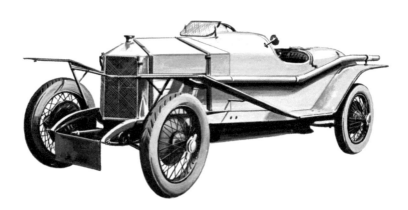

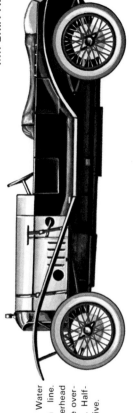

Imperia-Abadal, 1922. Belgium. Water cooled, four vertical cylinders in line. 80 × 149 mm., 2996 cc. Four overhead valves per cylinder, actuated by single overhead camshaft. Four forward speeds. Half-elliptic springs front and rear. Shaft drive.

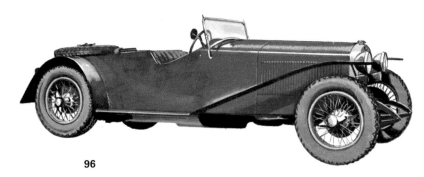

96

Excelsior Albert I, 1926. Belgium. Water cooled, six cylinders in line. 90 × 140 mm., 5350 cc. Overhead valves actuated by single overhead camshaft. Three forward speeds. Front half-elliptic springs, rear cantilever springs.

THE SPORTS CARS IN DETAIL

1 HORCH 18/22 PS, 1908, Germany

The way in which August Horch started his career in the motor industry can hardly have provided a less accurate forecast of what was to come: the man who became world famous for fierce sporting cars and later for luxurious *autobahn*-cruisers went as works manager to Benz of Mannheim, who were then (1896) renowned for feeble and conservative machines only a little less retrograde than the true horseless carriages of Gottlieb Daimler. Horch founded his own company in 1899, making his first car a year later. Serious production began in 1904. These early Horches were modest and conventional twins and fours with side valves in an 'L' head; but by 1905 the character of the Horch was changing, including big cars of up to 35/40 PS with overhead inlet-valve engines. Both the Horches of that year, the 35/40 PS and its smaller stablemate the 18/22 PS, were so powered. By now the Mercedes was the universal model for high-powered cars, but the two Saxons from Zwickau defied fashion and current technical thought by using shaft drive instead of chains. While Dr Horch was still in charge of the firm he launched—that is, until 1909—performance demonstrated in an active competition programme coupled with considerable technical sophistication was the watchword. One of each model competed in the 1905 Herkomer Trial, and an 18/22 PS won it in 1906 in the hands of Rudolf Stöss. Three special six-cylinder cars were built for the 1907 Kaiserpreis race. The 18/22 PS Horches for the 1908 Prince Henry Trial (illustrated) were remarkable not for their success (for they had none) but for their bodies, which were aimed at reducing wind resistance. Very low-hung, with horizontal, flared wings, the tops of the bonnet, scuttle and body forming an unbroken line, the crew sitting in exposed cockpits, these creations by Kathe of Halle caused a sensation, and were too extreme at the time to be followed.

2 BENZ, PRINCE HENRY TYPE, 1908, 1910, Germany

The famous line of spidery vehicles with their slow-turning horizontal engines and belt drive that had made the name of Benz of Mannheim ended finally in 1902, by which date they had become primitive throwbacks that no longer commanded a market. An interregnum when Marius Barbarou, who formerly worked for Adolphe Clément, was in charge of design was not a success; his cars were compromises, still too conservative and with nothing to distinguish them from numerous other mediocrities on the market. In 1904, with the appointment of Hans Nibel as works manager at Mannheim, that firm finally threw off its past and joined the mainstream of modern car design.

Nibel's normal production cars were conventional enough, with (at first) their side valves in a 'T' head, going over to an 'L' head layout in 1909, but retaining chain drive for the most powerful models without the option of shaft drive until 1908. In other words, the Benz according to Nibel conformed to fashion; they were beautifully made, big, and fast because they were big. The 40 PS of Fritz Erle and Edgar Ladenburg that won the 1907 Herkomer Trial was such a machine. However, the Herkomer Trials were already encouraging Benz, as they did so many other manufacturers, to produce more efficient engines. The 60 PS of 1906, an immense 9·8-litre affair, produced 70 b.h.p. with the help of overhead inlet valves, if only at 1300 r.p.m. It was classified as a 'Touren-und-Sportswagen'. This was a catalogued model. There were specialized Herkomer-derived varients of the 40 PS, of which the fastest was the 50 PS of eight litres' capacity. The upper of the two cars illustrated was an even more special Benz, built for the 1908 Prince Henry Tour. Long strokes were encouraged, resulting in the Benz's 115 x 160-mm. and 115 x 180-mm. engines. Both inlet and exhaust valves were overhead, and 100 b.h.p. was produced at 2000 r.p.m. Maximum speed was better than 85 m.p.h. Fritz Erle won in one of these formidable machines. The body illustrates the arrival of the 'torpedo' form in which attempts to reconcile reduction of wind resistance with the regulations of the Tour produced the basic elements of the sports-car shape that was to rule for twenty years. The diminutive, yet faired headlamps perfectly mirror the contradictory requirements of the event. The lower illustration shows a far cleaner line in the 1910 Prince Henry Tour Benz. Its 7·3-litre engine had four overhead valves per cylinder and gave 115 b.h.p. at 2100 r.p.m. This car

was faster than the sensational Austro-Daimler of that year (15).

3 OPEL 8 PS, 1909, Germany

By 1909, the date of the cars illustrated, the Adam Opel Motorwagen-fabrik was on the way to becoming Germany's biggest car producer, though their best days were to begin with the popular 'Puppchen' of 1912 and the postwar Laubfrosch. The Opel family had come far already: from when they started making sewing machines in 1862, and from the palmy bicycle days that followed. They, like most other German car makers, had begun car manufacture by using other people's designs—first the primitive Lutzmann of 1894 (a false start), then (from 1901) the hugely successful Darracq from France. By 1906 the Darracq connection had been dropped; the Opel had grown up, beyond dependence on foreign design. In the Opel-Darracq days, the firm had entered international competitions, albeit with no success. But 1907 saw the start of more serious sporting activity, and third and fourth places in the Kaiserpreis race. Opels competed in all the Herkomer Trials with vehicles of Opel-Darracq type, but the 1907 event also brought an entry from a new 18/30 PS 'German' Opel, a modern 'L'-head machine of of 4·7 litres with shaft drive, which was placed third. Opels were successful in hill climbs, too; but the most famous win of all was in the 1909 Prince Henry Tour, when the little 8 PS type shown carried off the honours. The formula this year favoured smaller, more efficient engines. Maximum speed was between 55 and 60 m.p.h., which was creditable for two litres and side valves. The car was subsequently offered as a catalogued model, as was usual. For the 1910 event, Opel entered some very different, very special machines with all-overhead valves and 100 b.h.p. from 7·3 litres. They were capable of 85 m.p.h., and were runners-up to the victorious Austro-Daimlers (15). The 1909 Prince Henry Opels, together with Fritz Erle's Benz of the same year and perhaps other competitors, were most important for their body shape, as is explained in the Introduction. The concave sides that resulted from exploitation of the regulations became the fashionable sports-car shape in central Europe for fifteen years, thanks to the success of the Opel and of the Austro-Daimler in 1910, and can clearly be seen in the upper illustration.

4 NSU 10/30 PS, 1912, 10/28 PS, 1909, Gemany

The Neckarsulmer Fahrzeugwerke followed German tradition in starting life making two-wheelers—bicycles and motor-cycles—and in passing on to building foreign cars under licence: in their case the Pipe from Belgium. In 1906 came the first native NSU product, a very modern four-cylinder light car with overhead valves and shaft drive. A team of three NSUs took part in the 1908 Prince Henry Tour. The lower illustration is of one of the 1909 Tour entrants, a 10/28 PS machine developed from the more touring 10/20 PS current from 1907 to 1910. The upper illustration shows the 10/30 PS of 1911-12, which carried a sporting

body but was the touring successor to the 10/20 PS, with the same cylinder dimensions but developing 30 b.h.p. at 1600 r.p.m., thanks partly, no doubt, to its overhead inlet valves and better breathing. Maximum speed was between 45 and 50 m.p.h.

5 SIZAIRE-NAUDIN, 1908, France

The Etablissements Sizaire et Naudin were one of the pioneers of what was to become regarded as the typical French sports car: usually cheap, strong, simple (though not necessarily conventional), light, stark of aspect, and fast for its size. Like the central European sports car of the same period, it evolved in competitions, in this case the Coupe de L'Auto or Coupe des Voiturettes, the Sicilian and Catalan Cups, and the Grand Prix des Voiturettes (see Introduction). Just as the German sports cars, as modified for public use, suited the German temperament, so the dashing little sporting voiturette fitted French fire and élan. The Sizaire-Naudin, new in 1905, designed by Maurice Sizaire and made by his brother Georges and the brothers Naudin, differed from the ruck in its adventurous yet highly successful technical specification. The power units were conventional enough, being (in their most characteristic guise) singles of De Dion inspiration and increasingly long stroke—the 1908 cars could be had with cylinder dimensions of 120 x 110 mm., 120 x 120 mm., and 120 x 130 mm., but by 1910 the stroke could be 140 mm., and the single-cylinder car in its final manifestation (1912) could be had in 70 x 140 mm. form. These were catalogued cars: the stroke of racing cars was elongated to as much as 250 mm. in 1908. The suspension, however, was anything but normal, being independent at the front by means of sliding pillars and a transverse leaf spring. The Decauville and the Ader had been seen with this layout before; but Monsieur Sizaire's transmission was even more idiosyncratic. There was direct drive on all three forward speeds, a movable ring on the propeller shaft engaging different sets of teeth on the final drive. The whole off-beat recipe was proved in the hardest school of all, when the Sizaire-Naudin carried off the Coupe de *L' Auto* in 1906, 1907, and 1908, and the Sicilian Cup in 1907. Clearly the suspension made up for what the armoured wood frame might have lacked in providing good road-holding.

6 COTTIN ET DESGOUTTES, 1911, France

The motor industry of Lyons, the second greatest centre of car manufacture in France after the Paris area, concentrated on heavier, more luxurious, more powerful and more expensive metal. Typical were the products of the Desgouttes concern, new in 1905 and renamed Cottin et Desgouttes in 1906. They started life making machines on tried German Mercedes lines. That illustrated was characteristic of its type: the biggest in the range in 1911. This particular car was geared for hill climbs, and weighed only 24 cwt. complete. Since the engine gave 110 b.h.p. at a leisurely 1600 r.p.m., it is not surprising that 100 m.p.h. was obtainable. The technical specification was conservative, including chain drive, and the car was a late example of a class that was on the way out: a modified racing car in concept, rather than a sports car proper, which was a newer, more specialized and more subtle type evolving from competitions (*see* Introduction). Unlike many Lyonnais makes, the Cottin et Desgouttes was little known outside France.

7 GRÉGOIRE 13/18 CV, 1911, 14/24 CV, 1913, France

The Grégoire was another make that made its name in the French *voiturette* competitions of the 1906–13 period. The firm began car manufacture as early as 1903, but their *voiturette* line started in 1905 with an 80 x 110-mm. 'L'-head monobloc twin of modern conception, less crude than many of the type. In 1911 the range still included the twin, but for several seasons a six and some fours had been offered beside it. The smallest four was the 13/18 CV shown in the upper illustration; a 2·2-litre machine whose engine developed 20 b.h.p. at 1600 r.p.m. Originally with three speeds only, by 1913 this car could be had with a four-speed gearbox. By that date, too, all models had monobloc instead of pair-cast cylinders. The next largest four (shown below, in 1913 form), was the better-known 14/24 CV of 3·2 litres, with a very long stroke. It developed 35 b.h.p. at the same engine revolutions, and had four forward speeds. The firm's racing *voiturettes* of this later period were quite different, with three-litre,

80 x 149 mm. 'T'-head engines, two carburettors, and dual ignition in 1911 and 1912.

8   ISOTTA-FRASCHINI TIPO KM, 1912, 1914, Italy

Cesare Isotta and Vincenzo Fraschini began in 1899 to import Renault and Mors into Italy from France, and two years later were assembling the first-named under their own name. The first wholly Italian-built Isotta-Fraschini seems to have been the 1902 24-h.p. on Mercedes lines; a big, powerful, expensive machine that set the company's style for the future. Its age of expansion began in earnest in 1905, with the finding of new capital, the opening of a new Milan factory, and the acquisition of Giustino Cattaneo, a brilliant designer. From 1907 to 1911, following the motor industry slump, the Lorraine-Dietrich company had a controlling interest, which meant that some details of some Isottas may have come from the drawing-board of Ettore Bugatti, who at the beginning of the period worked for the German branch of the firm. Four of the Maserati brothers worked at Milan in different capacities, too. Racing success came thick and fast, so all in all, it would have been surprising if technical innovations and sophistication had not followed. The car illustrated, the 100-h.p. Tipo KM. introduced in 1910, was a sports car in the sense that it was basically a racing car modified for road use—in that it incorporated the overhead camshaft configuration used in the 1905 120-h.p. racer, the 1908 10-h.p. Isotta, and the

$7\frac{1}{2}$-litre cars that were so successful in American races and popular there from 1908 to 1910. Thus it belonged to an earlier tradition, as exemplified here also by the Cottin et Desgouttes (6). Another indication of its lineage was its very large, slow-turning bi-bloc engine, and its chain drive. At the same time, it had the front wheel brakes introduced into the Company's cars in 1910, and its engine was most advanced for a catalogued car, with its shaft-driven overhead camshaft operating four valves per cylinder. Power output was up to 140 b.h.p. at 1800 r.p.m. Maximum speed was 90 m.p.h. One of the earlier versions with flat, rounded radiator is shown in the upper illustration, the body being an American-style speedster. The car below has a Germanic vee radiator and body. Beside the KM, which was first listed in 1912, was the Tipo TM, which had a smaller, monobloc engine but was otherwise similar.

9   SPA, 1913, Italy

The Società Ligure Piemontese Automobilie, more conveniently rendered SPA, was founded by Matteo Ceirano and Michele Ansaldi in 1906, and their first car appeared in the following year. Since Matteo had come from Itala, his first products bore more than a passing resemblance to the latter concern's machines, though this did them no harm. Every Italian make with a claim to public attention had to race, and SPA did so from 1907. Ernesto Ceirano finished third in the 1908 Targa Florio, and Francesco Ciuppa won the race in

1909. All SPAs were conventional, side-valve cars. That illustrated is the 25-h.p. sport, which had a maximum speed of around 75 m.p.h. The four-cylinder, 4·4-litre engine was cast monobloc, and there was a four-speed gear-box. In 1913 there were other cars in the range, all with shaft drive, all fours, and varying in size from 1·8 litre to 7·6 litres.

10 HISPANO-SUIZA ALFONSO XIII,
1914, 1911, Spain, France

The S. A. Hispano-Suiza, founded in 1904, was so called because its cars were designed by a Swiss, Marc Birkigt, and made in Spain. Birkigt concentrated upon expensive luxury cars, because there was little or no middle-class market for motor vehicles in Spain. He succeeded so well that the Hispano-Suiza became *the* Spanish make, patronized by the motorphile King Alfonso XIII. The king's name was given to the firm's first sports car, offered for sale from 1909; although its most familiar manifestation, with 80 x 180-mm. bore and stroke, as illustrated here, was not sold until 1911. In fact the Alfonso XIII Hispano was born and bred in the Spanish and French *voiturette* races, being derived from a line of cars that began with the company's entries in the 1909 Catalan Cup race: these were four-cylinder cars at a time when the single was still reigning supreme in such events, with a long stroke and side valves in a 'T' head and separate cylinders. The 1910 racing cars were similar, except for still longer strokes, while some had a bigger bore too. Power output was over 60 b.h.p. After 1910 Hispano-Suiza withdrew from

voiturette racing, but not before Zucarelli had won that year's Coupe de *L'Auto* race, with Chassagne third, and also came third in the Catalan Cup. The 'Alfonso', as shown in this book, continued unchanged through 1914, even though technically it had been outstripped not only by other makes but also by other Hispano models, which by now had overhead valves and monobloc engines. Such was the extent of their success. Some were built in the native Barcelona factory, and some assembled in the Paris works opened in 1911. Maximum speed in production form, with a chassis weight of only 13 cwt., was over 70 m.p.h. from about 55 b.h.p. Even the four-passenger type could better 60 m.p.h. Early cars had three forward speeds, increased to four in 1913, and a modern feature of what from the beginning had been an old-fashioned design was the unit construction of engine and gear-box.

11 STANLEY GENTLEMAN'S SPEEDY ROADSTER,
1907, 1908, U.S.A.

The Stanley, built from 1902 to 1924, was America's and the world's most popular steam car, and the longest-lived. Generally the Stanley twins, Francis E. and Freelan O., made touring cars, but in 1905–6 Stanley record-breakers were famous, carrying off the World's Land Speed Record in the latter year at 127·56 m.p.h. for the mile, and the firm listed a high-performance machine, the charmingly-named Gentleman's Speedy Roadster, illustrated, current from 1906 to 1910. Steamers already had a head start over gasoline cars in terms of acceleration, and the Roadster had a truly remarkable performance. The range of which it formed a part was born with the 10-h.p. Model E introduced in 1905, to which was added a 20-h.p. and a 30-h.p., with various styles of body. The 20-h.p. could be had in Roadster form, but the 30-h.p. Roadster was the most exciting model, weighing only 15 cwt. and capable of 75 m.p.h.

12 LOZIER 50 h.p., 1913, 1910, U.S.A.

Like so many motor manufacturers Harry A. Lozier started by making bicycles; then he moved on to marine engines. They had characteristics in common, notably high quality, longevity, and in the case of the marine engines, speed. When Lozier began selling cars in 1905, the same qualities were carried over into what was to become one of the finest cars of its day and nationality. Necessarily, it was also one of the most expensive; though Lozier advertising was a bit defensive about this. The first Lozier was a chain-drive 'T'-head four, but from 1908 there were two basic types, both with ball-bearing cranks and shaft drive: the four-cylinder 45-h.p. Type H, and the 50-h.p. Type I, a 9·1-litre six illustrated here. In 1911 they were renamed, respectively, Type 46 and Type 51. The chassis price of the latter in the same year was $5000 (then about £1000, which was more than was asked in Britain for the Rolls-Royce). In its last incarnation, as the Type 72 of 1913,

the big six had left-hand drive. It was also the last new Lozier model to have a ball-bearing crankshaft. With a two-passenger runabout body, maximum speed was better than 90 m.p.h. The make won the National Stock Car Championship in 1910, and came home second in the first Indianapolis 500 Miles Race of 1911; then it went on to win that year's Vanderbilt Cup Race. The most popular bodies on both sixes and fours were the sporting ones: the Briarcliff and Lakewood (lower illustration) sporting torpedos, and the Meadowbrook runabout (upper illustration). Running without road equipment, the Meadowbrook body was the Lozier racing style. Variants of the 'T'-head six, of lesser distinction, were a more modern, cheaper 'L'-head light six of 1909, the Model J; and the similar Type 77 of 1913. There was a more modest four in the following year, too (the Type 84), but all these attempts to combat growing lower-priced competition failed, and Lozier went out of business in 1918.

13 MERCER TYPE 35R, 1911, 35J, 1913, U.S.A.

The Mercer, so called after Mercer County, New Jersey, where it was built, was first made in 1911, and became famous with the coming of the Type 35 Raceabout. This was America's most famous speedster of all time, including even the Stutz Bearcat (14), though it was made for so short a period (1911–15). Initially it was powered by the breed's characteristic 'T'-head engine with four cylinders cast in pairs, which was replaced by a monobloc 'L'-head layout in 1915. Maximum power output was 58 b.h.p. at 1700 r.p.m., and top speed in stock form, thanks to a very high axle ratio, was just over 70 m.p.h. There was dual ignition. This engine was designed by Finley Robertson Porter. The earlier cars had three forward speeds; later ones had four, top being an overdrive, and a weight complete of little more than a ton. The competition successes of the Mercer were numerous, among the most important being victory in the race for the 1914 American Grand Prize. Mercers were third in the Indianapolis 500 Miles Race in 1912, and second in 1913. Twice they were runners-up in the Vanderbilt Trophy Race, in 1912 and 1914.

14 STUTZ BEARCAT,
1914, 1921, U.S.A.

Characteristically, the first car designed by Harry C. Stutz that was sold to the public was out of the common run: the American Underslung of 1905, a machine of extremely low build and clean lines. In the following year Stutz was working for the Marion Company, staying there until 1910. During that year he founded the Stutz Motor Car Parts Company, and built a car bearing his name for the Indianapolis 500 Miles Race. It only finished eleventh, but ran so regularly that it was given the label of 'The Car that Made Good in a Day' and was put into production. Three body styles were listed. There were many racing successes in 1912 and 1913, but it was not until 1914 that Stutz's most famous model appeared: the Bearcat speedster

shown in the upper illustration, which could be had with either a four- or a six-cylinder engine. Although so well known, the firm's racing successes henceforth were won not by the Bearcat, which was a typical American speedster of the time, not fast enough for serious competition, but by the advanced Stutz Wisconsin of 1915, a pure racing machine, with overhead-camshaft, sixteen-valve engine that developed no less than 131 b.h.p. The speedster was most usually seen with four-cylinder unit (also Wisconsin made), that had side valves in a 'T' head and pair-cast cylinders, and developed 60 b.h.p. at a modest 1500 r.p.m. The three-speed gear-box was on the rear axle. Harry C. Stutz left the company in 1919, and by 1921, when the car shown in the lower illustration was made, the Bearcat had been tamed almost out of recognition, as the picture demonstrates. It was by now much more a habitable sport roadster than a speedster in appearance. It was less adventurous mechanically, too: the gear-box was in a normal position behind the engine, which retained its archaic 'T'-head layout. The only major signs of modernization were the availability of a monobloc, six-litre engine in 1917 and the coming of detachable cylinder-heads in 1921. A complete redesigning took place in 1923, and the old car finally died.

15 AUSTRO-DAIMLER
PRINCE HENRY, 1914,
Austria

The Osterreichische Daimler Motoren Gesellschaft was founded in Wiener-

Neustadt in 1899 to make the German Daimler car in Austria-Hungary. From then until 1905 it was content to turn out, literally, Austrian Daimlers (as the cars were sometimes called when imported into Britain), but in the latter year Paul Daimler, who had been in charge, left. The young Ferdinand Porsche became head of the factory. With hindsight, it is reasonable to expect something exciting to have happened, but in fact nothing did for five years. The Osterreichische Daimler gained wider currency under Porsche, but this was because Emile Jellinek, Austrian Consul-General in Nice, who had mid-wifed the Mercedes into the world (originally a model of Daimler called after one of his daughters), now did the same for a model of Austro-Daimler called the Maja (after another daughter). Just as, at first, the Mercedes was only to be known as such in some European countries and the United States, so Maja was the name under which the car was known in America and Britain, and advertised widely, for Jellinek was a first-class salesman. One of the traditional Austro-Daimlers ran in the 1909 Prince Henry Tour, but it gave no hint of what was to come, with its side valves in a 'T' head. For the 1910 event, Porsche designed from scratch a team of cars that were built with the sole purpose of winning. It was worth doing so, for this year, the Tour was the most important single motor sporting event in the attenuated competition calendar. The design did not just 'happen': Porsche was no stranger to the principles of high efficiency engines, for he had already, in 1908, made an overhead-camshaft engine for airship use. In aviation

power units, it was recognized that high power, compactness, lightness and reliability was essential. Porsche's engine, of 5714 c.c., gave 95 b.h.p. at 2100 r.p.m. thanks to its efficient breathing as well as its considerable size. The four steel cylinders were separately cast. There were five inclined valves per cylinder, one inlet and four exhausts, all very large, actuated by a single overhead camshaft. The reciprocating parts were light, permitting the quite high engine revolutions produced. There was dual ignition, and maximum speed was about 80 m.p.h. Porsche was conservative in one respect: he preferred to transmit all this power to the wheels by chain drive. The importance of his design is not so much in its advanced nature alone (after all, the 1910 Prince Henry Benz [2] produced 115 b.h.p. from 7271 c.c., thanks to four overhead valves per cylinder, and was the faster car) but in the fact that it won general acceptance. This was partly because it gained the victory in an event of overwhelming importance with consequent world-wide publicity, and partly because unlike its most sophisticated competitors, it was completely reliable and practical, and could therefore be put into production for public consumption (in fact, 200 were made). This was the first time such a thing had happened with so advanced a design. The concave-sided bodywork was not original, having been devised by competitors in the 1909 event to take advantage of the rules. In the case of the Austro-Daimler it was designed by Ernst Neumann-Neander, who became Germany's most fashionable sporting body designer in the wake of the enormous *réclame* gained by the car. The machine illustrated was sold in 1914 to Prince Elias of Parma, and carried a specially devised Neumann-Neander body. Note that by this time (in fact in 1912), the Prince Henry model Austro-Daimler had lost its side chain drive.

16 AUSTRO-DAIMLER ALPENTYP, 1912, Austria

While one line of development, aimed specifically at winning the 1910 Prince Henry Tour, had resulted in the Prince Henry-model Austro-Daimler current from that year until 1914 (15), another line pursued by the company was to be just as successful. In the same year of 1910, Wiener-Neustadt introduced a modern small touring four with side valves in an 'L' head, its 80 x 110-mm. cylinders cast monobloc: the 16/18-h.p. Also in that year, the Imperial and Royal Austrian Automobile Club, encouraged by the success of the Prince Henry Trials, instituted their own International Alpine Tour, which came to attract, and to develop, a class of sports car that was efficient, elegant and as fast as it looked, but was not generally so complex as the Prince Henry cars had been, since speed was was not all-important. The car and the Tour came together in 1911, when the 16/18-h.p., now with lighter pistons, better breathing, an attractive aluminium sporting body, a shorter chassis, and a new designation—the 16/25-h.p., or 9/30 PS in Austria—won all the five major awards and the team prize. Power output was 30 b.h.p. at 1800

r.p.m. and maximum speed upwards of 60 m.p.h. The car shown here was put on sale as the Austro-Daimler Alpentyp. Prizes for clean sheets came the firm's way in the 1912 event, which was contested by new cars with bigger engines of 90 x 140 mm. This model, the 20/30-h.p., or 14/32 PS, was in turn available in 'Alpine' form as a result, though as late as 1914, the 16/18-h.p. and the 16/25-h.p. were still available as well. Outwardly they and the other Austro-Daimlers of touring origin differed from the 'Prince Henry' in having flat instead of vee radiators.

17 BUGATTI TYPE 13, 1910, 1914, Germany

Ettore Bugatti, one of the most famous manufacturers of competition cars of all time, was Italian by origin, but the Italian industry knew him only indirectly. True, he made his first car in Italy in 1898, but in 1902 it and its designer were taken over by the Franco-German firm of De Dietrich (or rather, by its German component, at Niederbronn). This company also took over a much bigger firm, the Italian Isotta-Fraschini concern, between 1907 and 1911, and at least three Isotta types of this period show Bugatti influence: the little 10-h.p. and the big Type KM and TM which appeared after Bugatti left to become a consultant engineer. He worked for Mathis of Strasbourg and Deutz of Cologne from 1905 to 1909, designing big cars. His first Deutz, at least, had his characteristic valve gear: overhead camshaft and curved 'banana'-shaped tappet blocks. Bugatti eventually joined Deutz full-time, being responsible for the 13/25-h.p. of 1909, which had still more in common with Bugatti's own cars that were to come. This, indeed, was the next step, Bugatti setting himself up in a small rented dyeworks at Molsheim in Alsac in the same year, with three ex-Deutz designers. The first Bugattis, five of them, saw the light in 1910. This was a remarkably efficient small four of advanced (though, as we have seen, amply foreshadowed) design. The four-cylinder, single overhead-cam-shaft engine had to propel only some 11 cwt. of motor-car in two-passenger form, but even so, 30 b.h.p. produced at no less than 3000 r.p.m. and a maximum speed of 60 m.p.h. from only 1·3 litres was astonishing for the date. It was comparable with the 20 b.h.p. at 2500 r.p.m. from 960 c.c. of the Apollo Type B Spezial (*see* [21]), of the same era. Although the Bugatti cost around double the price of other four-cylinder light cars, production was stepped up to 75 in 1911, to 179 in 1913, and about 500 in all were made before the First World War. By then there had been superficial changes: the original squared-off radiator began to give way to the familiar pear-shape in 1913, cam-shaft lubrication was more certain (though the engine's bottom end, sur-prisingly, was still splash-fed), and maximum speed had gone up to about 70 m.p.h. Longer versions were to be had, the Types 15 and 17, which had lower axle ratios and were intended for more formal bodywork, and before 1914, larger engines were shown as alternatives, with bores of 66 or 68 mm., giving 1368 or 1453 c.c. Early cars had single or double half-elliptic rear, springs, giving way to reversed quarter-elliptics in 1914. Naturally, the eight-valve Type 13 took a promi-nent part in racing, and although its most famous achievement was its second place in the 1911 French Granp Prix, it claimed fifty-seven wins be-tween 1911 and 1914, largely in hill-climbs on courses such as Gaillon and Mont Ventoux.

18 NAG TYP K5,
1912, 1914, Germany

The most celebrated model to come from the Neue Automobilgesellschaft before 1914 derived from the'L'-head monobloc four-cylinder machine that appeared late in 1907. This Typ N2, or Puck, produced 12 b.h.p. at 1500 r.p.m. Its development: the Typ K2 Darling could develop 18 b.h.p. thanks to its ability to rev up to 3000 r.p.m., a high degree of efficiency for the time (1911) from side valves. The indicated power was developed at 2100 r.p.m. The Darling, current until 1914, was winner of the Gothenburg Cup in the Swedish Winter Trial in 1912, 1913, and 1914. But the name of NAG had appeared in other competitions—the Herkomer and Prince Henry Tours, the Kaiserpreis race in 1907, the 1908 St Petersburg-Moscow race, the International Alpine Tours, and so on. The car illustrated is the Typ K5 of 1912–14, a bigger machine with pressure-lubricated en-gine giving 38 b.h.p. at 1750 r.p.m., and capable of between 55 and 60 m.p.h. It lent itself, as did other NAG models, to sporting bodywork of the kind shown.

19 MERCEDES 37/90 PS and 16/45 PS, 1913, Germany

In 1910, two new and very different lines of car were introduced into the Mercedes range, boosting the reputation of what was already the most distinguished, if rather conservative, passenger-car name in Germany. Three Knight double sleeve-valve-engined machines, all with live axles, culminated in the 16/45 PS. The first two were touring machines, but the last was developed into a chassis of considerable sporting potential, in its mildest form producing 40 b.h.p. 45 b.h.p. was also offered, and finally 50 b.h.p. at 1900 r.p.m. The car illustrated (below) developed its 45 b.h.p. at 1800 r.p.m., giving a maximum speed of between 50 and 55 m.p.h., but pure racing versions came second in the French Grand Prix, were fifth in the Indianapolis 500 Miles Race, and third in the Belgian Grand Prix, all in 1913. Although the 50-b.h.p. version was not listed until 1916, as early as 1910 three cars with this designation had carried off the first three places in the Czar's Cup event. Perhaps this is not so surprising, as a works 16/40 PS appeared at the Semmering hillclimb as early as 1909. In racing trim, the 16/45 PS was capable of nearly 80 m.p.h.

This car became one of the first Mercedes to bear the famous three-pointed star and, with the 37/90 PS, the first German car to wear the sharp vee radiator that was to become a trademark of the breed. The 37/90 PS (upper illustration) was a sports car in more traditional mould, since it had a poppet-valve engine and the side chain drive favoured by most powerful cars in that age. The engine was quite advanced in specification, with its three pushrod-operated overhead valves per cylinder (one inlet, two exhaust), although its $9\frac{1}{2}$ litres were called upon to produce their 90 b.h.p. at only 1300 r.p.m. By 1913 this had become 95 b.h.p., with a slightly enlarged bore. Sheer size and performance—75 m.p.h. —made the 37/90 PS the most spectacular and desirable car in the Mercedes range. Von Guttmann's 37/90 PS took home the premier award in the 1912 International Alpine Tour. The type's racing successes were gained mostly in 37/95 PS form, in 1914, when Ralph de Palma won the Vanderbilt Cup race and came fourth in the American Grand Prix; in the first instance averaging 77 m.p.h. for nearly 300 miles.

20 BUGATTI, 1913, Germany

Although Ettore Bugatti made his name with his small Type 13 and its derivatives (17), he had earlier made more large cars than small ones for other concerns, so it is not surprising to find him offering a big five-litre in 1912 and 1913. It had no type number, but Bugatti called it the 'Garros' after Roland Garros, the French aviator, who was a customer, and it was offered as the 19/100-h.p. in Britain. It had four cylinders and an overhead camshaft, but was otherwise notably different from the Type 13, with its chain drive, and three valves per cylinder instead of two. The weight was only 25 cwt., and power output was 100 b.h.p. at 2400 r.p.m., which gave 100 m.p.h. In its class, this was as remarkable a car as the Type 13, for its performance put it in the Grand Prix class, although it claimed to be no more than a sports car.

21 APOLLO TYP F REKORD, 1913, Germany

In 1910 the Automobilwerke Ruppe & Sohn AG, makers of the Piccolo air-cooled light car, became the Apollo Werke AG and started to make bigger, water-cooled machinery as well as air-cooled vehicles of one, two or four cylinders. In charge was Karl Slevogt, formerly of Cudell, Laurin-Klement, and Puch. He was not only an engineer, but also a competition driver, so it is not surprising to see him concentrating on sports cars with overhead valves, which took part in competitions between 1912 and 1914. His most re-markable design came in 1911, and was the Typ B of 4/12 PS, a very small and modern car with a one-litre four-cylinder engine in unit with the gear-box. In normal form it developed 12 b.h.p. at 1800 r.p.m., but it could turn at 2200 r.p.m., and in Typ B Spezial guise could be persuaded to produce 20 b.h.p. at 3000 r.p.m. This made it one of the most efficient power units in its class. Illustrated here is its sister model, the Typ F Rekord, which was of similar design but twice the engine size. The two-litre engine produced 28 b.h.p. at 2000 r.p.m., giving a maxi-mum speed of 60 m.p.h. Chassis weight was under 14 cwt., to which the two-passenger sports body added only another 2 cwt. The Rekord was current from 1912 to 1914. It was not surprising that the Baron de Vizcaya raced an Apollo, at a time when his brother worked for, and his father financed, Ettore Bugatti. The family were obviously connois-seurs.

22 AUDI ALPENSIEGER, 1914, Germany

When in 1909 August Horch left the firm bearing his own name that he had founded (1), he soon made a new reputation for himself with a car called the Audi, which was Latin for 'hearken', just as his own name was the German for the same word. His former associ-ates, who went on making cars, had prevented him from continuing to use Horch, so this was next best. The first Audi, the 10/28 PS, appeared in 1910, and carried on the sporting tradition of the 'Horch' Horches. The 2·6-litre 10/28 PS took part in the International Alpine Tours of 1911 and 1912, which had replaced the Prince Henry Tour as Europe's premier event for sports cars. In 1913 and 1914, when the new Type C 14/35 PS or Alpensieger sports model took part, the make qualified for the team prize. The 14/35 PS, which is illustrated here, could be had with an engine developing 35 b.h.p. at 1700 r.p.m., or 40 b.h.p., in the latter case providing the short-chassis cars with a maximum speed of well over 60 m.p.h. This car was made until 1921. The lay-out of the Audi was very similar to that of the 'old' Horch, with its over-head inlet and side exhaust valves.

23 ROLLS-ROYCE LONDON-EDINBURGH, 1911, 1913, Great Britain

Until 1914, Rolls-Royce (in spite of its unparalleled reputation for silence and refinement) was a name to be conjured with in competitions for road-going cars. Before he became associated with Henry Royce in the manufacture of cars bearing their names, C. S. Rolls had been a racing driver of note at the wheel of Mors, Panhard, Wolseley and other makes. Rolls-Royce had supported the 1905 and 1906 Tourist Trophy races, winning on the latter occasion, and set up a new record for the London–Monte Carlo run in the same year of 1906. The new Silver Ghost, introduced that year, did very well in the 1907 Scottish Reliability Trial and (more important) in the Two Thousand Miles Trial of 1908, which demanded a unique combination of reliability and high speed. 1907 saw the winning of the Royal Automobile Club's Dewar Trophy by the original Silver Ghost, for an observed 15,000-mile run with only one involuntary stop. In 1911 came an RAC-observed non-stop run in top gear throughout from London to Edinburgh, when over 24 miles to the gallon of fuel was obtained followed by a speed test on Brooklands Motor Course, where the car covered a lap at over 78 m.p.h. This was an all-round test, proving flexibility, economy, and speed. The performance was the more meritorious considering that the top gear-ratio used, 2:9:1, was high, and there were only three forward speeds in the gear-box instead of the normal four. (The first four-speed box had not been entirely satisfactory.) The car's body was one of the most beautiful ever made, light and narrow, with a tapered bonnet. The seven-litre, six-cylinder, side-valve engine, normally developing only 53 b.h.p. at 1700 r.p.m., was little modified: a higher compression and larger carburettor were the major

changes, giving about 58 b.h.p. This, incidentally, was the first Rolls-Royce to have cantilever rear springs. On some cars they were underslung. When the type was catalogued late in 1911, various body styles were fitted; even formal closed ones on occasion. The London–Edinburgh car that James Radley drove on the 1912 International Alpine Tour had a heavier-looking, uglier body than that worn normally. Nor was it a success in other ways: lacking a low enough bottom gear, it stopped on the Katschberg, shed passengers, and was disqualified. This humiliation resulted in a new, redesigned and improved four-speed gear-box being fitted to all cars. The London–Edinburgh was current until 1914, latterly with aluminium pistons,

24 VAUXHALL PRINCE HENRY, 1913, 1912, Great Britain

If the Rolls-Royce (23, 26) was Britain's best-known sports car abroad in the pre-1914 period, the most famous at home was certainly the C-Type or Prince Henry Vauxhall. Its evolution, which took place (like that of so many British sports cars of the age) in efficiency trials and on Brooklands Motor Course, began with the car that Laurence Pomeroy designed for the 1908 Two Thousand Miles Trial. A machine successful in this searching test would have to be reliable and practical as well as fast. The Vauxhall turned in the best performance, thanks to an engine that was tough as well as powerful: the 'L'-head side-valve unit of three litres' capacity produced 38 b.h.p. at a sustained 2500 r.p.m., then a high engine speed. It was achieved thanks to efficient breathing, light reciprocating parts, and a high compression ratio. The type was put on sale as the 16/20-h.p. and was further developed at Brooklands. By the end of 1909 the engine was giving 60 b.h.p. at 2800 r.p.m. In the following year a team of cars was prepared for the 1910 Prince Henry Tour. The 60-b.h.p. engine, with its steel pistons, high-lift camshaft and special valves, was fitted. A shorter, narrower and lighter chassis than that of the normal 16/20-h.p. carried a distinctive lightweight body with a sharp vee radiator (new on Vauxhalls). The cars were outclassed by such formidable competition as the Opels, Benzes, and Austro-Daimlers, but were capable of 72 m.p.h. The model was offered to the public from 1911 as the C-Type or Prince Henry model. It was somewhat detuned, with 55 b.h.p. on tap at 2500 r.p.m., providing 65 m.p.h. However, it was a works car with the more powerful engine, in the hands of Percy Kidner, that won its class in the 1911 Russian Reliability Trial for the Czar's Cup. Percy Kidner's car used in the 1912 Swedish Winter Trial was similarly powered. Fifty cars were made during 1912.

In that year, the production C-Type's engine was enlarged to four litres, now offering 75 b.h.p. at 2500 r.p.m., and since it was still in the original chassis, it gave the car a maximum of well over 80 m.p.h. The idea was to compete on more level terms with more powerful Continental sports cars; but the C-Type was soon to be superseded itself by the still more celebrated E-Type (73). In any case, its final incarnation was rather tame, since the bigger engine was mated with a longer, wider chassis designed for more comfortable bodies. Forty-three four-litre cars were sold.

25 AUSTIN DEFIANCE,
1912, Great Britain

Herbert Austin in his Wolseley days was a consistent supporter of motor racing, with cars entered in the Gordon Bennett races of 1902 to 1905 inclusive. These were specialized machines that bore little resemblance to the touring cars that made up the Wolseley range. When, from 1906, Austin started to make cars under his own name, he continued to build sedate, well-made, middle-class vehicles, but now his competitive efforts (at least until the 1920s) became patchier, and his competition cars were solidly based on his bread-and-butter line. The 1908 Grand Prix Austin was a tuned version of the six-cylinder 60-h.p. touring car, while the new 40-h.p. four-cylinder of the same cylinder dimensions formed the basis of the Brooklands racing Austin called 'Pobble'. From the 40-h.p. was derived Austin's first sports car. Its maker was one of the very few British manufacturers interested in exports to Russia at this time, and a 40-h.p. was entered in the 1910 International Tour for the Czar's Cup. The chassis was standard, its 'T'-head engine with separately cast cylinders developing a modest 42 b.h.p. from 5·8 litres, and pulling a body of conventional flush-sided design. However, it was subsequently offered to the public as the Vitesse type, for it made a non-stop run and collected the St Petersburg Automobile Club's Trophy. No Austin competed in the 1911 event, but the 1912 Russian Reliability Trial, with the Czar's Cup again at stake, saw a new 40-h.p. sports car in attendance. The touring car on which it was based was new late in 1911; the engine had a larger bore, giving 6329 c.c. Its designer, G. W. A. Brown, had been responsible for modifying a 15-h.p. Austin in that year for Brooklands use: this car, 'Pearley III', was a great success. His 40-h.p. sports car was called the 'Defiance'. Its engine was modified in respect of high-lift camshafts and a larger carburettor, and its body was a particularly handsome 'torpedo'. Until an accident wrecked it, the Austin seemed a certain winner of the Czar's Cup, for it must have been one of the fastest road cars of 1912. It was certainly the fastest in the Trial, in which 95 m.p.h. was claimed for it. It was timed at over 80 m.p.h. in the St Petersburg speed trials, and could exceed 67 m.p.h. in third gear. The 'Defiance' type (shown here) was offered to the public at the end of 1912, and it and the normal 40-h.p. were very successful in British speed events. The latter was dropped for 1913, and a new 30-h.p. substituted, but a 'Defiance'-type sports model was to be had on this chassis as well. It could see 75 m.p.h., but was slower than the four-litre Prince Henry Vauxhall (24) and the sports 25-h.p. Talbot (28), its main competitors, and cost a great deal more. The model was dropped, and both 'Defiance' and 'Vitesse' became no more than names for body styles.

26 ROLLS-ROYCE CONTINENTAL, 1913, and ALPINE EAGLE, 1914, Great Britain

The failure of the London-Edinburgh type Rolls-Royce in the 1912 International Alpine Tour (73) impelled the company to enter in 1913, using a car with a four-speed gear-box developed from the London-Edinburgh. Four machines participated, three of them works entries. They failed to win the team prize at which they were aiming, but C C. Friese's works car gained the most important single award, the Archduke Leopold Salvator's prize, and lost no marks at all. This time Rolls-Royce had made no mistake. Their cars were the largest and fastest in the Tour. The type was offered for sale as the Continental (upper illustration). Apart from its four-speed gear-box, it had a higher compression than hitherto, a larger carburettor, better cooling, brakes and ground clearance, a stiffer frame, and other improvements. It could, perhaps, be said that in 1913 the Rolls-Royce had no worthy opposition, but this was far from the case in 1914. Having proved their point, the factory did not enter again, but James Radley, the Rolls-Royce dealer who had made up the fourth in 1912, did so. He lost no marks, winning the prize of the City of Trieste. The Rolls-Royce put up the fastest time on the notorious Katschberg pass, and in the three-mile speed trial at Wels. It was sold to the public as the Alpine Eagle (lower illustration), in which form it was lighter than the Continental, had a still higher compression ratio, and could reach 85 m.p.h.

27 GN, 1920, 1913, Great Britain

From about 1910 to the immediately post-First World War years, after which he was offered something better, the would-be motorist who could not afford a 'proper' small car could have a cycle-car, at the cost of cramp, exposure, vibration, noise, a hard ride, crudity of construction and finish, usually unspeakable brakes and handling qualities, and sometimes mechanical temperament. The bonuses he got in most cases were economy of running, easy gear-changing (thanks to sliding-belt or chain-and-dog-clutch transmission) simplicity, strength, and a considerable performance, owing to the standard recipe of very low weight combined. with a lusty motor-cycle-type engine. The most successful of the breed in Britain was the GN, so called from the initials of its devisers, H. R. Godfrey and 'Archie' Frazer-Nash, whose first car emerged from its Hendon, London factory in 1910. Until 1915 and the end of civilian production, most GNs had two-speed belt final drive (which was prone to slip in wet weather), and their power output was limited, but post-war cars did better than their competitors because in addition to the cycle-car's usual advantages, they handled well, and they performed better, thanks to a basically sound engine specially designed for car use that was capable of development (the air-cooled 90 degree vee-twin), mated to three-speed chain transmission (available on some types from 1912–14). These qualities were reflected in a highly successful competition record which kept the name before the public eye. In 1921 alone, it won 112 first places in speed events. All GNs were really sports cars, in the sense that they were of sporting character (and were certainly bought exclusively by sportsmen in the widest sense)—even the so-called touring machines such as those illustrated, which had an inlet-over-exhaust-valve engine. The cheapest model of 1920, the Popular, weighed only 6½ cwt. and could reach 45 m.p.h. The next 'hottest' type was the Légère which had alloy pistons, and was good for 65 m.p.h., but was basically similar. The fastest GN was the Vitesse, with (in addition) all-overhead valves. In its final form, the Vitesse engine as sold offered ball-and-roller bearings, twin chain-driven overhead camshafts, alloy pistons, large inclined valves, and 35 b.h.p. From 1923 GN Ltd, foreseeing the end of the cycle-car boom in the face of competition from light cars (with most of the conveniences of the full-scale family machine) at much lower prices, toyed with shaft-drive chassis, sliding-pinion gear-boxes, four-cylinder water-cooled engines and other amenities of their dangerous rivals; but the last GNs of any sort were made in 1924.

28 TALBOT COMPETITION, 1914, Great Britain

In spite of its name, Clément-Talbot Ltd, was a British concern, although its cars were partly Gallic in inspiration until 1906. In that year, the new 20 h.p. Talbot appeared. It was wholly British in design, the creation of C. R. Garrard, the works manager. Its engine was outwardly conventional but of notably high efficiency, as was that of its 12/16-h.p. stablemate and the 15-h.p. that came later in the year. The latter two models in particular, by their phenomenal success in British hillclimbs and speed trials, earned the *marque* its slogan: 'The Invincible Talbot'. The 12/16's 2·7-litre, four-cylinder, 'T'-head engine could sustain 1500 r.p.m., which was high for 1906. For two seasons the make was almost unbeatable in its class, collecting 106 awards in 1907 alone. By 1908 the limit for sustained revs was 2000. One of the new 25-h.p. Talbots won its class in the Two Thousand Miles Trial of that year. For 1910, a new 25-h.p., a 4½-litre car with cylinder dimensions of 101 x 140 mm., had been introduced. Like its predecessor it enjoyed a fair degree of success in competitions, but for three seasons from 1909 the Talbot tended to be overshadowed by still more potent rivals. In 1911, however, G. W. A. Brown redesigned the 25-h.p., endowing it with an 'L'-head, in which form the model swept the board in 1913 and 1914. A sports model was offered to the public for the first time; it was called the SB or 'Competition' type, its engine developed 75 b.h.p. at 2500 r.p.m. instead of the normal 55 b.h.p. at 2000. it weighed only 25 cwt. complete, and it could exceed 80 m.p.h. A highly-tuned version of this unit, providing 130 b.h.p. at 3500 r.p.m., was installed in a 12-h.p. chassis to produce the celebrated machine that, in the hands of the works driver Percy Lambert, took the one-hour record to over 100 m.p.h. on Brooklands Motor Course in 1913. Another Talbot driver, Leslie Hands, used a replica of this formidable machine. In its ultimate

1914 form, these works cars had a stroke of 150 mm. and were the fastest things on the British road.

29 LANCHESTER SPORTING FORTY, 1914, Great Britain

In 1914 there came from the Lanchester Motor Company a machine utterly unlike anything produced by the company before, and (in appellation if not in specification) as unlike anything that followed it. A firm that had won fame in Britain for beautifully-made machines of extreme refinement and great inward and outward eccentricity, that had gained a limited but discerning clientèle mainly among the well-to-do, chauffeur-employing but sober professional classes, offered an equally well made but sporting car on almost conventional lines. The Sporting Forty, designed by George Lanchester, was a front-engined car with a normal hood, instead of carrying its power unit between the front seats as previously. This engine had side instead of overhead valves and a conventional jet carburettor in place of the familiar Lanchester wick instrument. Half-elliptic springs were worn at the front to complete a totally 'normal' exterior appearance, though Lanchester cantilever rear suspension did duty at the rear. The car also retained the traditional epicyclic transmission and worm final drive. The intention was to produce a car that would appeal to a wider public than its predecessors; the 'Sporting' appellation was intended to attract the owner-driver. It was, in fact, quite fast, being (it was said) capable of averaging 50 m.p.h. from London to Liverpool and attaining 70 m.p.h. from its 78 b.h.p., developed at a modest 1800 r.p.m., in spite of a weight of 38 cwt. It handled well, too. Only six cars were built before civilian production ceased in 1915, but the type formed the basis of the highly successful post-war Forty, which although boasting an overhead camshaft, 95 b.h.p. from a somewhat larger engine, and certainly an equal performance, was never called anything but a luxury tourer.

30 MORGAN GRAND PRIX, 1915, Great Britain

Until 1934 the British motorist who was willing to put up with discomfort and noise (invariably), and with crudity and mediocre brakes, handling and performance (usually), could bene-fit from a taxation scale which favoured the three-wheeler as well as from the simplicity and low initial cost of such vehicles. Some three-wheelers were better than others, and the best—and thus the most popular and long-lived —was the Morgan. Conceived in 1909 and offered to the public by H. F. S. Morgan in the following year, it was simple enough but it was by no means crude, with its sliding-pillar and coil spring front suspension and tubular backbone frame. It used a one- or two-cylinder J.A.P. air-cooled engine of motor-cycle type driving the single rear wheel through dog clutches and chains, one for each forward speed. It held the road better than its competi-tors, which was just as well, since it weighed only three cwt. and it was fast, with 55 m.p.h. available. The first

cars were single-seaters with tiller steering, which must have been really perilous. By 1911 wheel steering had arrived, though this was geared direct and had to be treated circumspectly. One might have thought that this specification was exciting enough, especially since by the end of 1913 the make had won more awards than any other machine in the cyclecar class, but in 1914 came the Grand Prix model illustrated; the company's first cata-logued 'sports' variant. Its appearance was prompted by the make's win in the Amiens Cycle-car Grand Prix of 1913, with a water-cooled vee-twin of 996 c.c., at an average speed of 41·9 m.p.h. The type remained in the catalogue as the only sports Morgan until 1919, the only major change being the availability as an option of a Swiss MAG engine of 1096 c.c. in water or air-cooled form. For 1920 came the more famous Aero Morgan, supplementing and eventually replacing the Grand Prix.

31 CUNNINGHAM 1919–20, U.S.A.

Some people hold that the vee-eight Cunningham was the finest car to come out of America. Certainly this exclu-sive luxury machine, made (not, for the most part, assembled) in small numbers by James Cunningham Son & Co. of Rochester, New York, from 1916 to 1933, was beautifully built, and lovely to look upon. Its owners paid for their exclusiveness, too, to the tune of $9000 (then £1800) in its latter days. Its side-valve 7·2-litre engine had eight cylinders in vee formation, and alumin-ium was used for pistons, cylinder head and crankcase as well as for the bodies. In its early years the big Cunningham engine developed 90 b.h.p. at 2400 r.p.m., but this rose to 110 b.h.p. at 2500 r.p.m. later. 'European' features, usually found only on expensive cars in America, included a four-speed gear-box and detachable wheels as standard. The 1919-20 Speedster, which is illustrated here, was a very fast car, being capable when running stripped of a sustained 90 m.p.h.

32 KISSEL 6-55, 1924, 8-75, 1927, U.S.A.

Although (in common with most manufacturers of speedsters) the Kissel Motor Car Company of Hartford, Wisconsin made touring cars as well as more glamorous machinery, they were far better known for what was one of the best of the assembled speedsters, both in looks and quality. It was all the more unfortunate that the first, made in 1917, had to be burdened with the name of Kissel Kar Silver Special Speedster, which sounds like something out of Tom Wolfe. 'Kissel Kar' was at that time the name applied to the make, and 'Silver Special' derived from Conover T. Silver, the New York distributor of the make, who was responsible for the handsome styling of the Silver Special range, which were Kissel Kars with his touring or speedster coachwork. The New York Show of January 1918 saw a chrome yellow speedster on display, and this colour was standardized for speedsters in 1919. Henceforth all Kissel speedsters were popularly called 'Gold Bugs'. The dummy outside exhaust pipes of early

examples were soon dropped. So, from 1919, was the name Kissel Kar, all future cars being plain Kissels. The first speedster engine, the 6-45, was a six made by Kissel, of 4·7 litres' capacity and developing 61 b.h.p. at 2300 r.p.m. The cylinder head, pistons, and connecting rods were alloy. The top gear acceleration—a walking pace to 60 m.p.h. in 30 seconds—was very good. The chassis was dropped at front and rear. The three-quarter-elliptic rear suspension was replaced by half-elliptic springs in 1921, while three years later came the 6-55 engine, with a marginally shorter stroke. It was current until 1928. In 1924, external contracting Lockheed hydraulic four-wheel brakes were to be had as an option. For 1925, an eight-cylinder engine could be had—the 8-75, most of it made by Lycoming. It was current through 1927, and developed 71 b.h.p. at 3000 r.p.m. It appeared in the speedster in 1926. The eights culminated in the 8-80 and White Eagle speedsters of 1928, of which the latter had a maximum speed of 100 m.p.h., from 115 b.h.p.

33 SORIANO-PEDROSO 6/8 CV, 1920, France

In spite of its name, this was a French car; though at one time it did hail from as close to the Spanish border as Biarritz, and its makers, de Soriano and the Marquis de San Carlos de Pedroso, were certainly Spaniards. It was unusual for a *voiturette*, too, in that it used a multi-plate clutch instead of the more normal cone, and unusual for any post-war car (on the Continent, anyway) in having chain drive. The four-cylinder side-valve 6/8 CV engine, made by Ballot, of one version (shown here) had dimensions of 60 x 100 mm. (1130 c.c.), but there was also a 1590-c.c. Ballot engine mated with a four-speed gear-box inserted in a roomier chassis that was equipped with a differential. A sports version of the former had a fractionally smaller bore of 59 mm., to bring it into the 1100-c.c. class. The maximum speed was between 65 and 70 m.p.h., which was extremely creditable. The Soriano-Pedroso was made from 1920 to 1924.

34 HINSTIN S.U.P., 1921, France

Jacques Hinstin was one of the army of small constructors who began making sporting *voiturettes*, mostly in the suburbs of Paris, after the First World War. Offered between 1921 and 1926, it was seen with proprietary engines of various origins, which was normal: either a 62 x 91-mm., 1100-c.c. CIME, or the 59 x 100-mm., 1095 c.c. Ruby, both with four cylinders and push-rod operated overhead valves. Power output was 20 b.h.p. at 3000 r.p.m. in the former case, and there were three forward speeds. Front suspension was by a single transverse spring. Helped by the absence both of front wheel brakes and a differential, the chassis weight of early cars was little over 5 cwt. Maximum speed was over 62 m.p.h. The origins of the make and its later ramifications are confusing, but it seems that the cars of Hinstin, who had been the Paris agent for Grégoire, were made in the Grégoire works at Poissy and may have been derived from that

make. This theory is supported by the fact that the Hinstin, which was supplied to several firms in France and appeared under different names there, was called the 'Little Greg' in Britain. It seems also to have been one of the many obscure French cars sold by Gamage's store in London at different times under their name.

35 SÉNÉCHAL, 1921, 1925, France

Robert Sénéchal, later a Delage racing driver, set himself up in Courbevoie in 1921 as a maker of small sporting cars for the French minimal motorist. They were not easily distinguishable from the majority of their fellows, with their proprietary engines, absence of a differential, and transverse front suspension with quarter-elliptics at the rear. The first (of which one is shown in the upper illustration in 1921 Gaillon Hill Club form) Sénéchal used a four-cylinder side-valve Ruby unit of 903 c.c. and had only two forward speeds (which *was* unusual), but by 1922 all models fitted the norm, with a three-speed gear-box. At this time the Sport was a side-valve car, while the Grand Sport had pushrod overhead valves in a slightly larger engine. In 1923 the o.h.v. car had a 59 x 100-mm., 1094-c.c. power unit, and could reach 70 m.p.h. By 1925, cars could be ordered with both four forward speeds and front-wheel brakes and could be persuaded to reach 85 m.p.h. in racing trim; the alternative TS3 Sport still had 3 speeds, rear-wheel brakes only, and higher final drive ratios. It is shown in the lower illustration in 1925 form. The make won the Bol d'Or race three years running: in 1923, 1924, and 1925. By that time (1925) the firm had been taken over by Chenard et Walcker, but continued to make cars until 1929.

36 BIGNAN, 1922, France

Jacques Bignan, like so many of his compatriots, was really only interested in sporting cars; but he was a good deal more original than most. He progressed from making engines for other people's cars to offering his own. This Bignan of 1918 produced 50 b.h.p. from three litres of side-valve engine, which was not at all bad. This car and its developments might be fast (70 m.p.h.), but they were conventional. The same could not be said for the Causan-designed two- and three-litre models in 1922, in which a single overhead camshaft operated two valves per cylinder in the more touring machines, and four (with two plugs per cylinder) in the true sports models. The two-litre sports car was built experimentally in two examples with desmodromic (positively-closed) valves, in which form (shown here) it won its class in the Belgium Grand Prix at Spa in 1922, and in 1924 took the world's 24-hour record. Its power output and revving capabilities were remarkable for any two-litre of its day other than a pure racing car, which it was not; 70 b.h.p. at 5000 r.p.m. Maximum speed was nearly 90 m.p.h. The design was not persisted with; instead, the car was given an overhead camshaft operating four valves per cylinder through rockers. In this form, it won its class in the Le Mans 24-hour Race of 1923 (coming third overall), and at

Spa in 1924. Power output was 75 b.h.p. at 4500 r.p.m. in the car's original form, with 96 m.p.h. available, this later being increased to 80 and then 85 b.h.p. (with twin carburettors). There were brakes on the front wheels and transmission only. The machine as sold to the public, the Grand Sport, was capable of 85 m.p.h.

37 BUGATTI BRESCIA TYPE 23, 1922, France

In 1914, the Type 13 Bugatti (17) was made (though not yet sold) with four valves per cylinder instead of two, for racing purposes. A team of three cars was built for the 1914 Grand Prix des Voiturettes, which never took place. They had the 66-mm. bore engines already mentioned, giving 1453 c.c. After the war, the Bugatti make's nationality changed from German to French, with the cession of Alsace to France. The cars were finally revealed in 1920, when they won the Grand Prix des Voiturettes at Le Mans. Their fame was assured by their triumph in the Italian Voiturette Grand Prix the next year, which was held at Brescia. Friderich's car won at 72 m.p.h. The model was forthwith (unofficially) christened the Brescia (although in fact it gained 172 wins between 1920 and 1924), and was sold with plain- or with ball-bearing crankshaft. About 1700 of both varieties were made up to 1926; with front wheel brakes from 1925. The Type 13 had the shortest chassis. The intermediate-chassis car was officially dubbed the Type 22, and with long chassis, the Type 23. From 1922 they had a bore of 69 mm. and 1496 c.c.

Though the origins of the Types 22 and 23 lay in the pure racing 16-valve Type 13s, and these production cars could be and were used for racing, most wore sports or touring bodies. Their performance and handling qualities were legendary. Maximum speed depended on weight and gearing, but a typical Type 23 with fairly habitable bodywork could hold 70 m.p.h. and was good for perhaps 75 m.p.h.

38 DALILA, 1922, France

Bouquet er Cie made the charmingly-named Dalila *voiturette* from 1922 to 1924. It was typical of its breed in most respects, with its proprietary engine, in this case a small side-valve four by Ruby. The first Dalila's engine had a 55 x 95-mm. bore and stroke with 902 c.c., and was rated at 10 CV but had a true output of around 15 b.h.p. There were two forward speeds on this model, but then a type with a 57-mm. bore and 962 c.c. appeared, which had a three-speed gear-box. The really unusual feature of the make was its suspension, which was independent by an articulated lever to each wheel, the levers being linked to two quarter-elliptic springs, one each side of the chassis. The top speeds of the two versions were around 40 m.p.h. and 45 m.p.h. respectively, but some pretty little sports models (illustrated here) were made for competitions.

39 HISPANO-SUIZA H6, 1922, H6C, 1926, France

The most glamorous and exciting of the luxury cars of the 1920s was, by common consent, the H6 Hispano-Suiza. This car, which first appeared from the works of the French company at Bois-Colombes in 1919, established the primacy of the French offshoot of what had started life as a Spanish concern (10) by virtue of its swiftly-spreading and all-conquering name. It was the first Hispano developed in France, and was the sole model emanating from Paris until 1930; the company relied on it entirely. It was made in Spain, but in far smaller numbers, as that was a comparatively poor country, that never could support a luxury vehicle of its own for long. Nothing like it had been seen before. Here was a machine with two of the main attributes of the luxury car (flexibility and comfort), even if it lacked silence; yet its specification, performance and handling characteristics were those of the fiercest competition machines combined with one they too seldom enjoyed: real reliability. The explanation lay in the design, which was the most modern in the world. The engine, like those of other manufacturers who were to follow but never seriously rival the Hispano, was derived directly from its makers' wartime aero engine experience, with the demands on efficiency and stamina at high speeds that that implied. A single shaft-driven overhead camshaft actuated two overhead valves per cylinder. There were two plugs per cylinder. Reciprocating parts were light: the pistons were alloy, and the connecting rods tubular. Though the cylinder head was fixed, the six 100 x 140 mm. cylinders were aluminium, with steel liners. The crankshaft was pressure-lubricated, and ran in seven main bearings. Power output, from 6·6 litres, was 135 b.h.p. at 2750 r.p.m., which was double that of conventional luxury cars of the day, mostly pre-war designs. With such power, low-speed torque was impressive, enabling three forward speeds to be combined with a high axle ratio. A minimum of gear-changing was called for, rendering the car very suitable for town work, while it could also cruise at high speeds when engaged in long-distance touring—its two main functions. Maximum speed was 85 m.p.h., which was better than most out-and-out-sports cars, but at the same time, the Hispano could accelerate from a fast walking pace to 50 m.p.h. on top gear in 21 seconds. The chassis matched the performance. Light but rigid (customarily a contradiction in terms), it was furnished with extremely powerful servo-assisted four-wheel brakes, another revolutionary feature in 1919. Yet, by 1924, the lily had to be gilded, for the H6 had stronger competition by then. The result was the H6C Sport or Boulogne model, shown in the lower illustration, which had a bigger bore, eight litres, a maximum speed of 110 m.p.h., and a shorter chassis if required. It derived its name from wins in the Coupe Boillot races at Boulogne in 1921, 1922, and 1923. In the first race, the normal engine dimensions were still being used. The 1922 cars, bored out to provide 6860 c.c., also won the Autumn Grand Prix at Monza. The 1923 machines were a full eight litres, and accounted for a class win in the San Sebastian Touring Grand Prix as well as the Coupe Boillot. In all, 2614 examples of the H6 and its derivatives were made up to 1938.

40 BRASIER TC4,
1923, 1924, France

Brasier, or to be exact Richard-Brasier (as the car was called from 1902 to 1907) was a famous name indeed in sporting circles in that period, for it won the Gordon Bennett Trophy for France in both 1904 and 1905. From 1908 until the 1920s, however, the company lost interest in competitions. The staple line from Ivry-Port until 1927 was a range of rather too expensive fours of 2·1 and 3·4 litres and no distinction, that did nothing to prevent their manufacturers' gradual slide into oblivion. Brasiers had acquired front wheel brakes, unit-construction gearboxes and pushrod-operated overhead valves by 1923, but in this they merely followed fashion. However, there was also in that year the TC4, which was a modified version of the 2·1-litre TB. It had an extremely robust, five-bearing crankshaft, a higher power output, two plugs per cylinder, and wire wheels. This car was entered in the Le Mans 24-hour Races of 1923 and 1924. As can be seen from the illustrations, it was quite a handsome machine that betrayed little of its pedestrian ancestry, and circulated regularly, if unspectacularly at about 48 m.p.h. to finish seventh and eighth in the latter year.

41 BENJAMIN P2, 1923, and BOL D'OR TYPE, 1925, France

The Société Benjamin's *voiturette* of 1921, hailing from Asnières, had a smaller engine than most of its type. The 4 CV unit, made by Lemâitre et

Gérard, was a four-cylinder side-valve of only three-quarters of a litre, developing 11 b.h.p. at up to 2500 r.p.m. Maximum speed was around 40 m.p.h. The three-speed gear-box lived on the rear axle. About fifty of this Type A were built. It and its successors (the Type B, etc.) did better in tests of endurance like the Bol d'Or (lower illustration), than in pure speed events. A three-passenger car followed in 1923, the Type C; by this time the power output had risen to 14 b.h.p., and there was also a true sports model with an overhead-camshaft engine turning at 4500 r.p.m. It was capable of over 60 m.p.h. Experiments in 1924–5 with two-stroke engines resulted in the two-cylinder P2 of 6 CV (upper illustration) and the three-cylinder P3 of 9 CV. They failed, and the firm reverted to standard practice, this time using Chapuis-Dornier engines of 5 CV and 7 CV. Liquidation followed in 1926, and an attempt to revive the firm with a new name, Benova, applied to the 7 CV car, failed.

SCAP and Ruby. The SCAP engine used at first was a 5 CV of 900 c.c. with side valves, in unit with a three-speed gear-box. Its only unusual feature, for this type of car, was the rear suspension by cantilever springs. The Sport was fitted with an overhead-valve Ruby engine of 972 c.c., developing 25 b.h.p. at 3400 r.p.m. Its top speed was between 55 and 60 m.p.h., while the Super Sport could exceed the latter figure comfortably. A class win in the 1923 Tour de France prompted the appearance of a 'Type Tour de France', which was, however, not particularly sporting; indeed, its body was more comfortable than that of the true sports models. From 1927 there followed a different modern line of ultrasporting cars with sharply-raked radiators, very low build, and quarter-elliptic rear suspension. The fiercest was a Cozette-supercharged 1100-c.c. machine, with o.h.v. SCAP engine. With 60 b.h.p. on tap, it could exceed 100 m.p.h. Unsupercharged, power output was 35 b.h.p.

42 BNC, 1923, France

Jacques Muller built a light two-cylinder *voiturette* under his own name from 1921 to 1923. In the latter year, a new firm was born, Bollack, Netter et Cie, and a new works was opened. Muller, with Messrs Bollack and Netter providing the finance, began to make four-cylinder cars under the name of BNC. The basic model was available in a variety of forms, from delivery truck to Super Sport. Strong and economical, it relied on the well-tried four-cylinder proprietary units sold to constructors by

43 AMILCAR TYPE CC, 1923, France

The Société Nouvelle pour l'Automobile was founded in 1920 in the Paris suburb of Saint Denis to make sporting *voiturettes*, as were so many other little concerns at the same time. Joseph Lamy and Emile Akar, financiers, provided the money, while the engineering knowledge came from André Morel and Edmond Moyet, formerly of Le Zebre. Their object was to provide simplicity, strength and dependability as well as lightness and economy, so they left technical complexity and reliance on proprietary parts to others. The first Amilcar, the Type CC of 1921, illustrated here, developed 18 b.h.p. from a 903-c.c. four-cylinder side-valve engine of the company's own manufacture. The crankshaft had only two bearings, lubricated by splash feed. In common with other cars of the breed, the Amilcar lacked a differential, and wore quarter-elliptic springs front and rear. Weight was only $8\frac{1}{2}$ cwt. with the normal two-passenger body, so 50 m.p.h. was to be had. From 1922, permutations on the CC design were also offered. The CS was a true sports car with a one-litre engine developing 23 b.h.p. and allowing up to 60 m.p.h., while the CS3 was the same car with a three-seater body. The C4 was a longer version of the CS, less highly tuned, designed for roomier bodies. All three types were sold until 1924, when they were supplanted by the CGS. From 1922 they gained an enviable sporting reputation, won first by their victory in the first 24-hour race for the Bol d'Or that year. In both 1922 and 1923, they won their class in the famous Circuit des Routes Pavées race. Success in such gruelling events confirmed the new make's stamina.

44 SANDFORD, 1924–25, France

Two French manufacturers built the British Morgan (30) under license: Darmont, and Sandford. The latter started by copying the original designs, but to a limited extent. The Sandford had three wheels, chain drive, a tubular frame, and independent front suspension; but from the beginning used a four-cylinder engine in conjunction with a three-speed sliding-pinion gearbox, and soon progressed to more sophisticated things. First came front wheel brakes, and then, in 1926, a wheel at each corner and shaft drive; but independent front suspension and a tubular frame were retained. With a supercharged Ruby engine of 1088 c.c., developing 50 b.h.p. at 4000 r.p.m., these machines, still very light, were a formidable proposition indeed. Various other Ruby engines were used: a 985-c.c., with 24 b.h.p. and variations of a 1097-c.c. unit up to 35 b.h.p.

45 BALLOT 2LS, 1924, France

Like the Duesenberg brothers, Ernest Ballot made engines for other manufacturers, and also racing cars, before he built passenger cars for sale—the second from 1919, the third from 1921. Like the Duesenberg, too, the Ballot benefited from the publicity gained by its racing brethren—the three-litre, eight-cylinder cars were fastest in the Indianapolis 500 Miles Race in 1919 and 1920, and in 1921 second in the French Grand Prix and first in the Italian Grand Prix. The first Ballot passenger car was the 2LS in the upper illustration. This was in fact the two-litre, four-cylinder, sixteen-valve, twin o.h.c. racing car that had taken third place in the French Grand Prix, 'detuned' for road use by fitting a less anti-social exhaust system and a self-starter. Power output was 75 b.h.p. at 4000 r.p.m., and the maximum speed 92 m.p.h.—figures which reveal the car's racing character, for they were unheard of in two-litre road cars in 1921. Not surprisingly, the market for this very fierce, very expensive car was limited, and fewer than 100 were made. They were designed by Ernest Henry, who had been responsible for the famous racing Peugeots of 1912–14.

46 BUGATTI TYPE 30,
1924, 1925, France

The Type 30 Bugatti shown here was Ettore Bugatti's first serious attempt to make a comfortable touring car. Coming when and where it did, in 1923, it took the form of a fast tourer in the French idiom. It was remote in purpose from the 16-valve Type 13 and its derivatives the Types 22 and 23 (37), which were basically sporting *voiturettes* and quite unsuited to long-distance touring whatever body they carried. The Type 30 differed technically, too, in that it had only three valves per cylinder (as did all future Bugattis until 1931)—two inlet and one exhaust. Unfortunately the Type 30 was not a homogeneous design. The three-litre, eight-cylinder engine, which was fundamentally two four-cylinder, $1\frac{1}{2}$-litre blocks end to end, had a crankshaft with only three main bearings and was not quiet, smooth or reliable enough to attract the intended customers. The performance was there (75 m.p.h.) but the stopping-power was not, for although the Type 30 became the earliest Bugatti to have four wheel brakes as standard, those at the front being at first hydraulically operated, they did not work well. The whole thrown-together design had

a blight on it, since the Grand Prix Bugattis of 1922–3 that were the basis of the Type 30 had been almost as unlucky, and ugly as well, with their experimental streamlined bodies. The Type 30 was developed into the similar Type 38 in 1926, but this was not a much better car. It was not until the following year that a really satisfactory medium-sized touring machine came from Molsheim, in the shape of the fine Type 44. The importance of the Type 30 is historical only, in that in its day it was the smallest eight-cylinder car ever to have been in serious production.

47 CHENARD-WALCKER
TYPE X, 1924–25, France

The best-known competition cars of Chenard et Walcker were the four-cylinder machines, notably the 1100-c.c. 'Tank' (57), but in 1924 and 1925 an eight-cylinder was also offered, in sports form only, the Type X. Its basis was the four-cylinder, single overhead-camshaft two-litre car of 1921, of which the engine was simply doubled. The vertical camshaft drive was between the two-blocks. The resulting unit produced 130 b.h.p. The car appeared first in the 1924 Le Mans 24-hour Race, where after setting up a new lap record at 72 m.p.h., it retired. Like the two-litre car, this machine had large brakes on the front wheels, but none on the rear, as was the case with other French makes. The straight-eights which were built in 1925 (three of them only) differed from the 1924 machines in important respects. They were lower, they had brakes on all four wheels, and they were alleged to be capable of no less than 112 m.p.h. Nevertheless, the two competing cars once more retired at Le Mans; though their name was to some extent salvaged by a win in the Belgian Grand Prix at Spa.

48 D'YRSAN, 1924, 1927, France

The firm of Cyclecars D'Yrsan of Asnières, started by Raymond Siran, was one of the few *voiturette* makers in France to espouse the three-wheeler— only Darmont and Sandford (44) did so otherwise, and both of them followed the British Morgan model (30). The D'Yrsan was a much more complex, if heavier, vehicle, with more modern conveniences such as water-cooled four-cylinder engines, three-speed gearboxes, plate clutches, shaft primary (though chain final) drive, and front wheel brakes from the beginning, which was in 1923. The D'Yrsan had a tubular chassis and independent front suspension, as did the others, but the latter was on different lines, with two superimposed transverse springs. The tamest model used an overhead-valve Ruby engine of 972 c.c., giving 20 b.h.p., which propelled the 7-cwt. tricycle at 60 m.p.h. There were faster types. One, that ran in the Bol d'Or Race, used a 62 x 90-mm. unit of 1088 c.c. that could be had Cozette-supercharged; while another had a side-valve Ruby engine of 750 c.c. (57 x 95 mm.). The fastest of Siran's three-wheeled creations was good for 85 m.p.h. After 1927, he concentrated on four-wheeled cars, as the three-wheeler had no future in France.

49 MAJOLA TYPE DT, 1925, France

Sporting *voiturettes* of advanced design had been emerging from Monsieur Majola's Saint-Denis factory since 1911; indeed, he had made an overhead-camshaft unit in 1908, to the design of Doutre. The pre-war Type B was succeeded by the Type F (with 62 mm. bore instead of 59 mm, and 1088 c.c.) in 1922. The bigger model concurrent with it was the Type DT (65 x 105 mm., 1390 c.c.). This car, which is illustrated here, had its origins in the first Majola of 1911, the Type A. With longer-stroke engines, a team was entered in the 1914 Grand Prix des Voiturettes, which never took place, but they did run in the 1920 race. They could reach 80 m.p.h. but only finished fourth. The Type DT had the same engine dimensions, and was capable of around 80 m.p.h. All these cars had a chain-driven overhead-camshaft engine and ball-bearing crankshaft. They were more sophisticated than most vehicles of their kind in other ways, too; with their four forward speeds and half-elliptic springs all round. There was also a Competition model. In 1927 came Majola's swansong, an air-cooled four with only three forward speeds and lacking a differential, but then the firm was absorbed by Georges Irat.

50 MARGUERITE TYPE BO, 1925, France

The Marguerite first emanated from Courbevoie in 1920. Not many (about 250) were ever built, but one was the earliest racing mount of Raymond

Sommer, the racing driver. The first, the Type A, had a two-cylinder engine made by Train, but its successor, the Type B and its developments, were altogether more serious machines. The Type B used a side-valve Chapuis-Dornier engine of 900 c.c. The BO5 was a touring car, as was its variant the BO7, which had more generous chassis dimensions for carrying bigger bodies. The Type BO (shown here) which was initially given a side-valve engine of 59 x 100 mm. (1094 c.c.) from the same supplier, and had no differential, was quickly endowed with an overhead valve unit that gave a maximum speed of around 72 m.p.h.; but some of the racing cars had three valves per cylinder, in which form they could exceed 80 m.p.h. The last of the breed were extremely handsome, low-hung competition cars, the Type BO2, made in 1927–8 under the name of Morano-Marguerite.

51 VOISIN C5, 1925, France

On the face of it, the first Voisin did not seem likely to give birth to a line of formidable, expensive fast tourers in the best French tradition—Gabriel Voisin started motor manufacture by acquiring the rights in an 18 CV Knight double sleeve-valve engine from André Citroen, who had the design from Panhard and was going to use it himself, but dropped the idea. In other words, the basis of the Voisin was a type of engine not then renowned for its high efficiency, bought from the man who was to be France's foremost manufacturer of cheap economy cars. However, this four-litre Type C1,

which had aluminium pistons, was eventually developed into a competition car which won the Grand Prix de Tourisme in 1922 and in that year, attained a power output of 150 b.h.p. at 4000 r.p.m. Reverting to production types, the normal model was capable of over 80 m.p.h. in top gear and 65 m.p.h. in third, with 80 b.h.p. at 2500 r.p.m. Meanwhile, alongside the C1 there arrived the C3, which was a sporting variant. The full sports-car version was the C5 illustrated here, introduced in 1923. It had tubular connecting rods– and magnesium pistons to increase the available revs. The ports were enlarged, and the compression ratio raised. This engine produced 100 b.h.p. at 2700 r.p.m. The radiator was lowered, the brakes were given vacuum servo assistance, and half-elliptic rear springs replaced the cantilevers worn by the C1. In spite of the size of these cars, they were not as heavy as would be expected, since Voisin was a fanatic for lightness. They handled well, and were notably flexible and silent: not characteristics usually associated with sports cars at the time. This car beat the famous Blue Train from Paris to Nice by six hours.

52 TALBOT TYPE 2SC, DC, 1925, France

Automobiles Talbot of Suresnes was the firm from which, under another name, the famous Darracq had come since 1896. When the Société Alexandre Darracq gained control of the British Clement-Talbot concern (makers of the British Talbot car) in 1919, the name was appropriated and applied to the French Company and car (though not in Britain, where British Talbots continued to be made, and where the French car was still called a Darracq or a Talbot-Darracq, to make the distinction clear, since the latter was still sold in Britain). The first French Talbot cars sold were a fine if short-lived vee-eight, and a 14 CV of prewar design of which a sports version was made. Late in 1920 there appeared a modern car, the 1506-c.c. 9 CV, with four cylinders, overhead valves, and (until 1926) a three-speed gear-box in unit with the engine. It was called the DB. The sports model of 1922 had a power output of 39 b.h.p. at 3000 r.p.m., a bore of 68 mm. giving 1·6 litres, higher compression, a bigger carburettor and altered valve timing. It was capable of up to 70 m.p.h. in top gear with 45 m.p.h. in second (so did not suffer unduly from lack of a fourth speed), and handling was good. This larger, 10 CV engine was named the DC. In 1926 the car in DD Sport form had a four-speed gear-box and 1·7 litres, after being bored out to 70 mm. It went out of production in 1928. The lower illustration shows a sedan, and the upper, one of the special cars that took part in the Le Mans 24-hour Race in 1925. This Type 2SC had a shortened stroke of 103 mm. to bring it within the 1500-c.c. class. The 2SC was unsuccessful at Le Mans, but gained class wins in such gruelling events as the Circuit des Routes Pavées.

53 GM, 1925, France

La Société Gendron & Michelot of Paris were one of many small-scale assemblers of small cars, which differed from the general run mainly in looking much more substantial. It was made in 1100 c.c., 1200 c.c., and 1500 c.c. form, in all cases with four-cylinder engines by CIME. A $1\frac{1}{2}$-litre sports car, the GC2, was listed in 1925. This had a single overhead-camshaft developing 48 b.h.p., which, it was claimed, provided a maximum speed of 75 m.p.h. One of the two cars (illustrated here) entered in the Le Mans 24-hour Race of 1925 finished at an average speed of over 45 m.p.h. From 1926, only the smaller cars were made. Two of the 1100-c.c. machines, with special twin o.h.c. engines, competed at Le Mans in that year.

54 EHP, 1925–26, France

The Etablissements Henri Précloux, first of Courbevoie and then of Colombes, another Paris suburb, made their *voiturettes* from 1921 to 1929; the usual span of the type. In most respects it was just as conventional in its design, too. The first cars were powered by a four-cylinder, side-valve Ruby engine of 900 c.c. (1095 c.c. and pushrod overhead valves for true sports cars), with a three-speed gear-box, front suspension by a single transverse spring, rear quarter-elliptics (apart from some early cars, which had cantilevers), and no differential. By 1926, CIME engines were being used (four cylinder, 1200 c.c.), and half-elliptic front springs could be had. As was common, the firm made very different, much fiercer machines for racing. Those entered in the 1925 Grand Prix de Tourisme had four-cylinder, 1496-c.c., single overhead-camshaft engines, four-speed gear-boxes, and underslung frames. Similar cars were entered for the Le Mans 24-hour Race the same year (upper illustration). They were offered to the public in three forms: MI, MIS, and MIC (the last being supercharged). At Le Mans in 1926, the car reappeared with shorter chassis and 'Tank' style streamlined bodies (lower illustration). Also as usual, the company built solid touring cars towards the end of its life: a range of CIME-engined sixes of between one and two litres capacity.

55 LORRAINE-DIETRICH 15 CV SPORT, 1925, 1926, France

Lorraine-Dietrich was a name famous for fast cars and for competition successes well before 1914: in 1906 it won the Circuit des Ardennes, and in 1907 the Moscow–St Petersburg race; a 1912 Grand Prix Lorraine-Dietrich took world records at Brooklands Motor Course. After a war spent making aero engines, the technical director Marius Barbarou prepared two very modern new touring sixes: the 15 CV and the 20 CV. The 15 CV was an inexpensive machine intended for the middle-class family man, and being up-to-date, was American in appearance, controls, and to some extent design. Its $3\frac{1}{2}$-litre six-cylinder engine was built in unit with a three-speed gear-box with central lever. It had aluminium pistons, and ignition was by Delco coil. Top speed was 57 m.p.h. Oddly, the pushrods of the overhead-valve gear were at first

exposed, and were extremely thin. The car had good acceleration; it was very reliable; it held the road well; and its steering light and precise, so further potential was there. As an indication of its quality, the touring car was continued basically unchanged until 1932. From 1924, the year in which all models acquired front wheel brakes, the 15 CV was to be had in Sport form as well, with short chassis, twin carburettors, dual ignition, larger valves and servo brakes. This was one of the finest as well as one of the best looking sports cars of its day, offering not only high performance but also extremely good brakes and a high standard of flexibility, even though a four-speed gear-box only arrived in 1928. In the 1924 Le Mans 24-hour Race a 15 CV was second; in 1925, the car of de Courcelles and Rossignol won outright; and in 1926, Bloch and Rossignol duplicated the achievement, averaging over 66 m.p.h. Maximum speed of the Sport model was nearly 90 m.p.h.; the Le Mans cars were capable of about 95 m.p.h. Among other triumphs, the 15 CV came second in the Belgian Grand Prix at Spa in 1925. The Sport was offered until 1930. In its last two seasons, it could be had with cabriolet or sports sedan coachwork as well as open bodies.

56 BALLOT 2LTS, 1926, France

Ballot's touring car, the 2LT, was introduced alongside the ferocious 2LS (36) in 1924. This, designed by F. M. Vadier, was one of the finest and most modern fast tourers to come out of France, and when first seen, it had no competition in its class. Its four cylinders had the same dimensions as those of the 2LS, but there was one overhead camshaft, operating two valves per cylinder. There were front-wheel brakes from the beginning, to cope with the 70-m.p.h. performance. They were later given servo assistance. Road-holding and steering were excellent. In late 1924 a more sporting variant was to be had, as the 2LS was dead: this was the 2LTS, with inclined valves and hemispherical combustion chambers. Both types were replaced in 1928, after 2000 of the 2LT had been made. The pistons were aluminium. Coil or magneto ignition could be supplied, and the gear-box had a central ball change.

57 CHENARD-WALCKER, 1926, France

The first Chenard-Walckers to show symptoms of a sporting tendency were the four-cylinder, 2·6-litre and three-litre side-valve fast tourers of 1920, of which the former, by 1921, could be had with a two-litre single overhead-camshaft engine suitable for competitions. Brakes were on the front wheels only, servo-assisted. One of the three-litre cars, in overhead-camshaft form, won the first Le Mans 24 hour Race in 1923. Still better known, however, were the redoubtable 1100-c.c. competition machines designed by Touté, which won their class at Le Mans in 1925, the Coupe Boillot at Boulogne in 1926, and their class in the same year's Spanish Grand Prix. The four-cylinder pushrod overhead-valve engine was

sometimes supercharged by Cozette, although the crankshaft had only two main bearings. There was an auxiliary rotary exhaust valve in each cylinder. Apart from their performance, which earned them the title of 'The Invincible Chenards', their most remarkable feature was their appearance, thanks to their slab-sided, all-enveloping so-called 'Tank' bodies reminiscent of those used by Bugatti and Voisin. An outwardly similar but much 'cooler' type was offered to the public. Maximum speed of the sports-racing cars was 95 m.p.h. unsupercharged (as illustrated), with 55 b.h.p., while the supercharged machines were good for 107 m.p.h. The company abandoned racing in 1927, but astonishingly, put their works cars back into racing ten years later. They were entered unsuccessfully in the Le Mans race of 1937, but went on to win that year's Bol d'Or Race.

58 RATIER, 1926, France

The Ratier from Montrouge, made by a firm better known for airscrews, was a latecomer on the *voiturette* scene, arriving only in 1926; nor did it stay long. It was unusual in several ways which made it more interesting than many of its contemporaries. It was one of the first serious four-cylinder sports cars to be sold to the public that had an engine in the 750 c.c. class. It was much more sophisticated in design than most, though it lacked a differential. The single overhead-camshaft unit was capable of very high sustained revolutions and therefore of an excellent power output. Unsupercharged, it produced 34 b.h.p. at 5000 r.p.m., but furnished with a Cozette supercharger, 46 b.h.p. at 5500 r.p.m., or no less than 61 b.h.p. at 6000 r.p.m., were available. Unfortunately, this fine little engine was burdened with a three-speed gearbox; but this was insufficient to explain the Ratier's small part in history—the latter was due to the fact that its makers were concentrating on aviation work, and ceased production after only a handful had been put together.

59 SCAP 6CV, 1926, 1927, France

The Société de Construction Automobiles Parisiennes of Billancourt was unusual in that, as well as being well known among French assemblers for its proprietary engines, it made complete cars in great variety, if small numbers. Pre-war cars (1912–14) had Ballot engines in different sizes from 8 CV to 15 CV, did well in competitions, and were offered in sports form. After the First World War, however, the firm concentrated upon *voiturettes*, mostly side-valve fours of conventional specification except for their rear suspension, which was by a single transverse cantilever spring centrally pivoted on the chassis in conjunction with two linked half-elliptics. None made any impression until 1926, when a new range appeared. These had normal half-elliptic suspension and pushrod overhead-valve engines. The four-cylinder cars could be had either in 6 CV (7 CV in 1927), 1100 c.c. form, or as the 8 CV of 1200 c.c. The former engine produced 24 b.h.p. and the latter 26 b.h.p.

at 3200 r.p.m., and were both sold to other constructors as well. The 8 CV was a touring chassis basically, but sedan, cabriolet or sports bodies could be had on both that and the 6 CV. Maximum speeds varied according to engine and body, but were between 65 and 78 m.p.h., which was very creditable. However, there was also a special 1100 c.c. engine, furnished with the bore of the 1200 c.c. machine but with a shortened stroke and a Cozette supercharger. This was installed in a short chassis, and the ensemble was said to be capable of over 100 m.p.h.

60 SALMSON GRAND SPORT, 1926, 1927, France

The Société des Moteurs Salmson of Billancourt, aircraft engine makers, started their motor manufacturing life, like Sandford (44) and Darmont, by importing a British cycle-car design and making it under licence; in this case the GN (27), which had an air-cooled vee-twin engine. Twins were sold from 1919 to 1925, but by 1921 Salmson were converted to fours. One, the more famous though not the first to appear, was a twin overhead-camshaft water-cooled four of 1100 c.c. designed by Emile Petit, dropped into the GN frame together with a normal three-speed (later four-speed) sliding-pinion gearbox and shaft drive instead of the GN's dog clutches and chain drive. This formidable little half-ton car won the 1921 Grand Prix des Cycle-cars. A more substantial chassis followed, with half-elliptic front springs and the original quarter-elliptic still at the rear; though there was still no differential. Power output was 33 b.h.p. at 3800 r.p.m. in 1922 form. In 1923, 1924 and 1925 Salmsons won their class in the Brooklands 200 Miles Race. They took home the Biennial Cup in the Le Mans 24 hours Race for 1926–7 and 1928–9, and twice won their class in the Targa Florio Race. Production models were available from late 1922. The Type D was a tourer. Its truly sporting derivations came in three types: the Grand Sport (1926), which had three forward speeds, a two-bearing crankshaft and (at first) splash lubrication of the bottom end; the Grand Sport Special (also 1926), which had a four-speed gear-box and a pressure-fed three-bearing crankshaft; and the Grand Prix, which had the twin-plug San Sebastian-type engine further modified in respect of an optional Coziette supercharger, and a three-speed gear-box. Even the Grand Sport could exceed 70 m.p.h. For clients in search of less excitement, there was at the same time the pushrod overhead-valve car, which was also of 1100 c.c. but was notable for having only four pushrods (or rather, push-and-pull rods) and four rockers to actuate its eight valves. This, the Type AL, has been offered to the public in 1921, before the twin o.h.c. car arrived. It acquired its half-elliptic front springs for 1923, and front-wheel brakes in 1926. In 1927 the AL, too, could be had as the Grand Sport (three speeds) and Grand Sport Special (four speeds) in its more exciting manifestations. The last year of the AL was 1929, and of the twin-o.h.c. cars, 1930.

61 CEIRANO TIPO CS, 1921, Italy

The Giovanni Ceirano S.P.A., founded by the member of the famous family who had been responsible before the First World War for the SCAT (one of which had won the 1912 Targa Florio Race) and the Rapid, concentrated on fast tourers and pure sports cars. That illustrated was the first Ceirano sold, the Tipo CS of 1920–4. It was not intended as a sports car—its side-valve 2·2-litre engine claimed only 22 b.h.p. at a modest 2000 r.p.m.—but it was seen with odd sporting bodies of the kind shown (characteristic of Italy), which look unfinished but which are in fact complete, if doorless. The true sports versions were the Tipos CS2 and CS4, with a bigger bore (78 mm. instead of 75 mm.) and $2\frac{1}{2}$ litres. A CS2 won the 1922 Alpine Cup. Its maximum speed was 78 m.p.h. There was also a hotter variant of the CS2, the CS2H of three litres (with an 85-mm. bore), which was seen in pure racing form in such races as the Targa Florio, and which could reach 84 m.p.h. The CS4, for its part, was inwardly very similar to the normal CS2.

62 SPA, 1921, 1922, Italy

SPA was a make that had established a sporting reputation before 1914, notably in the Targa Florio race (9), and they preserved it after peace came. There were two basic side-valve touring models between 1921 and 1928 (though in fact they were quite expensive fast tourers rather than the bread-and-butter middle-class machines implied by the name): the 2·7-litre Tipo 23 with four cylinders of 85 x 120 mm.; and the similar but six-cylinder Tipo 24, with 85 x 130-mm. bore and stroke and 4·4 litres. A sports version of the first was made, the Tipo 23S, offering 45 b.h.p. at 3000 r.p.m., but it was not specially fast (around 75 m.p.h.); the sports variant of the bigger car was better known, and is illustrated here. It had two overhead camshafts, four valves per cylinder, tubular connecting rods, alloy pistons and cylinders with steel liners, a detachable head, twin carburettors and front wheel brakes: a most sophisticated design for 1921–2. Some examples had sharp vee radiators and high, rather ugly Germanic bodies with faired-in tops, while others used a gentler vee reminiscent of the RLS Alfa Romeo (68); indeed, the whole car, which was fast but big and heavy, was in the same class.

63 ANSALDO TIPO 4CS, 1923, Italy

One of the pleasantest sporting tourers to come out of Italy was the two-litre, four-cylinder Ansaldo. Its ancestor, the first car made by Automobili Ansaldo, a division of the country's biggest engineering works, was the 1800-c.c. car of 1921, with a bore and stroke of 70 x 120 mm., an overhead camshaft, and aluminium pistons. Power output was about 36 b.h.p. at 3000 r.p.m. It was soon dubbed the 4A. The 1·8-litre four carried the prefix '4' to the end of its days (as the 4F) in 1928. The sports derivative (of the 4C) was the 4CS illustrated. This had cylinder dimensions of 72·5 x 120 mm., giving 1981 c.c.,

48 b.h.p. at 3500 r.p.m., and (from 1923) front-wheel brakes. Maximum speed was a guaranteed 65 m.p.h. Later, some touring models were endowed with the two-litre engine, too: the last one was called the 4H. Ansaldos were remarkable in that they all used the single overhead-camshaft layout: nothing more pedestrian was ever offered. The big fours were quite successful in competition, winning the Coppa Ciano in 1921 and 1923, even though none of them ever had more than three forward speeds.

64 FIAT TIPO 501S, 1924, Italy

The first car to be designed for quantity production by Italy's biggest motor manufacturer was bound to make a powerful impression, and so it was with the Fiat Tipo 501. The earliest examples were on the road in 1918, but the new car was first shown to the world at the 1919 Paris Salon. Unlike so many lesser firms at the time, Fiat did not make the mistake of cutting costs by foisting an excessively stark and spindly, fragile lightweight on the public. The 501, designed by Carlo Cavalli, was an exceedingly solid machine of generous dimensions for its class. A four-cylinder side-valve engine of 1460 c.c., developing 23 b.h.p. at 2600 r.p.m., made in unit with a four-speed gear-box, was fitted. The finish was mediocre and the lines were unhandsome, which did not much matter in the home market, and the car was undergeared, which was expected in Italian conditions, but being Italian, it was pleasanter to drive than most vehicles of its type. The steering, gear-change and handling generally were good, and the maximum speed of around 50 m.p.h. was creditable for the day. It would take any amount of the punishment that these virtues, and the Italian driving temperament, implied. In 1925 front-wheel brakes became available, not before time, and were standard when in 1926 the car was renamed the Tipo 501B. Many people wanted a faster 501, which could be achieved by fitting such home conversions as the Silvani overhead-valve head (available from 1924), providing 35 b.h.p. and up to 78 m.p.h., or by buying the Tipo 501S (which is illustrated) instead. The latter's engine produced 26 b.h.p. at 3000 r.p.m., which was not much improvement over the normal car, but bodies were very rakish and, in the case of the *torpedo speciale* by Ghia in the lower illustration, most elegant as well.

65 CHIRIBIRI MILANO, MONZA NORMALE, 1925, Italy

Chiribiri & Co. of Turin, constructors of aero engines as well as motor vehicles, were unusual on the Italian motoring scene of the 1920s in that while they made some so-called touring cars, their bias was firmly towards competitions. Antonio Chiribiri's basic post-war machine, intended as a low-priced utility car, was a 1·6-litre side-valve four, which by 1923 had a shorter stroke (65 x 112 mm. instead of 65 x 120 mm.) that brought it within the 1500-c.c. class. By then it was called the

Milano, and by 1925 had front wheel brakes. Power output was 20 b.h.p. at 2800 r.p.m. (upper illustration). The fiercest Chiribiris were the pure racing cars, which do not concern us here but are worth a passing mention to emphasize the firm's leanings. The first was made in 1921, but in the following year there appeared close copies of the twin overhead-camshaft two-litre Fiat Grand Prix cars of 1921, though with only four cylinders, of which the power output eventually reached 83 b.h.p. Tazio Nuvolari drove one of these cars, which were good for 110 m.p.h. More relevant are the sports variants of the Milano, the Monza Normale which could be had blown or unblown, giving 45 b.h.p. at 3500 r.p.m. in the latter case (lower illustration), and the Monza Spinto, which was a truly ferocious lightweight supercharged machine producing 65 b.h.p. at 5000 r.p.m. and nearly 95 m.p.h. Both had single overhead-camshaft engines. There was also the so-called Grand Prix model, which was in fact a fast touring car differing little from the Milano.

66 CEIRANO TIPO N150S, N150, 1925, Italy

In 1924 a successor to the Tipo CS (61) appeared, in the form of the Tipo N150. Current until 1930, it was a machine of different concept, designed for the more sporting fringe of the light-car market, with 1½ litres and four cylinders. The side view (below) is of the normal side-valve model, offering 30 b.h.p. at 2800 r.p.m. The other view (above) is of its faster variant, the Tipo

N150S, which had front-wheel brakes from the start, wire wheels, and a pushrod overhead-valve engine of the same dimensions. Brakes and road-holding were excellent. This N150S was sold in Britain as the Newton-Ceirano by Newton & Bennett Ltd. Power output was 40 b.h.p. at 3500 r.p.m., giving a maximum speed of over 60 m.p.h. A racing version with a twin overhead-camshaft engine was made. The N150 and N150S provided Giovanni Ceirano with his only real commercial success, but he did not have the resources to exploit it.

67   DIATTO TIPO 20, 1925, Italy

The S. A. Autocostruzioni Diatto of Turin had been making cars since 1907, at first under French Clément licence. The Tipo 20 of 1924-6 (introduced at the 1923 Paris Salon) was not the first Diatto to show promise of a sporting temperament, the 2·7–litre side-valve 4DC of 1919 having that distinction, but the former was far better known. Its single overhead-camshaft four-cylinder engine, of two litres' capacity, gave 45 b.h.p. at 2700 r.p.m., and it had a four-speed gear-box and front-wheel brakes from the beginning. Top speed was about 62 m.p.h. Rather more exciting was the Tipo 20A which had aluminium pistons, and produced 52 b.h.p. at 3100 r.p.m. It could exceed 70 m.p.h. In 1926 came the basically similar but shorter Tipo 30. Alfieri and Ernesto Maserati produced a supercharged twin overhead-camshaft engine developing 75 b.h.p. at 4500 r.p.m. and providing about 100 m.p.h., some

of which were fitted into the 20A sports chassis. In such a car, Alfieri Maserati first made his name.

68   ALFA ROMEO RLSS, 1925, 1927, Italy

The S. A. Lombarda Fabbrica Automobili made French Darracqs under licence until 1910, when they began to build cars under the name of A.L.F.A. The first sports cars produced by their designer, Giuseppe Merosi, were hotter versions of his three side-valve fours of 2·4, 4, and 6 litres—the 15/20-h.p., 20/30-h.p., and 40/60-h.p.—made before and after the First World War. When peace came, the make was renamed Alfa Romeo, since Nicola Romeo had assumed control in 1915. These models, of which the most successful were the 40/60-h.p. and the final development of the 'middle' car, the 20/30 ES Sport, did extremely well in national competitions, particularly in the Targa Florio Race, in which they came second in 1920, and won their class in 1921. However, by 1922 the old machines had been supplemented (later replaced) by two new cars of more modern design, with six cylinders, three litres, and pushrod overhead valves. The touring RLN (later RLT) started life with a bore of 75 mm. and a flat radiator. The RLS, the sports-touring version, differed from it mainly in having twin carburettors, a higher compression ratio, a 'hotter' camshaft, lighter connecting rods, a shorter chassis and the 76 mm. bore (providing 2994 c.c.) that only the later tourers had. There was also a vee radiator, found on a few of the latter. The RLS differed, too, in having front-wheel brakes from the word go. Power output was 71 b.h.p. at 3500 r.p.m., permitting a maximum speed of about 75 m.p.h. Its development, the RLSS of 1926–7, illustrated here, had dry-sump lubrication, and produced another 12 b.h.p. and another 10 m.p.h. The fiercest version of all was the ultra-short Targa Florio or RLTF, which was smaller, lighter and more powerful (80 b.h.p.). The name was appropriate, since Alfa Romeo chalked up yet another success in the 1923 event, winning it outright with a 3·1-litre, 95-b.h.p. version. There was also a 3·6-litre car developing 125 b.h.p. and capable of 112 m.p.h. The latter two machines were never catalogued. In all, 929 examples of the RLS family were made.

69 ISOTTA-FRASCHINI TIPO 8ASS, 1926, Italy

After the First World War, the Fabbrica Automobili Isotta-Fraschini made no more pure sports cars like the ferocious Tipo KM and TM (8); nor, indeed, more than a single model—the six-litre Tipo 8, a superbly-made car for the carriage trade. The chassis and transmission were conventional enough, but the engine was not. It was the first series-production straight-eight in the world, and it was of sophisticated, if not advanced, design. The cylinder block and the pistons were aluminium, the latter running in steel liners; there were pushrod-operated overhead valves, tubular connecting rods, and two carburettors. Although this was not a fast-revving

engine (the maximum power of 75 to 80 b.h.p. was developed at only 2200 r.p.m.), the crankshaft had nine bearings, wore a vibration damper, and was pressure lubricated. The stresses were low, and reliability was high. The gearbox, made in unit with the engine, had only three forward speeds, no more being thought necessary for what was intended as a top-gear car. Front-wheel brakes, which some Isottas had had since 1910, were standard. Maximum speed was 70–80 m.p.h. according to bodywork, and contemporaries were impressed by the car's road-holding and braking. However, unfavourable comparisons were drawn with the H6 Hispano-Suiza (39), the Tipo 8's main Continental competitor, which had a bigger, more powerful engine, was lighter, and handled better still. The outcome was first a Sport version of the Tipo 8, and then a new luxury car, the Tipo 8A, with 7·3-litre engine (achieved by enlarging the bore from 85 mm. to 95 mm.), up to 120 b.h.p. at 2400 r.p.m., higher gearing and better brakes. But the Hispano was still the more impressive car, and became even more so when the H6C Sport was introduced. Isotta riposted in 1926 with the car illustrated, the fine Tipo 8ASS, or Super Spinto. The engine had a higher compression ratio, larger valves, better breathing arrangements, and a power output of up to 150 b.h.p. at 2800 r.p.m. There were still higher and closer gear ratios, and although a complete four-passenger car still weighed 48 cwt., which was little or no improvement on the touring Tipo 8A, maximum speed was a guaranteed 100 m.p.h., and 80 m.p.h. could be reached in fractionally over 25 seconds. Buyers could have the normal Tipo 8A chassis length, or a shorter one. The Tipo 8ASS was made until 1928. Unlike its Hispano-Suiza rival, neither it nor its variants, even in the hands of drivers of the calibre of Count Aymo Maggi and Bindo Maserati, won important competition successes outside its native land.

70 CALTHORPE SPORTING FOUR, SUPER SPORTS, 1920, Great Britain

Before the First World War, Calthorpe were the earliest and most consistent, if not the most successful, British supporters of the Coupe de *L'Auto* races in France. Like so many other manufacturers of family cars, they catalogued a sports model, too; but after peace came the latter was the only sign of sporting temperament left in the firm. The basic Calthorpe was the 10-h.p. light car, which in its class was fast, exceptionally handsome, and extremely well made. It provided a good basis for the sporting variants which by now even more firms felt they had to offer—in the case of Calthorpe, they were to be had with rounded and pretty two- or four-passenger bodies in polished aluminium. A mildly-modified Sporting Four was followed by a Super Sports type, for which a maximum speed of 60 m.p.h. was guaranteed, thanks to the free-revving ability of an engine tuned in respect of drilled and balanced aluminium pistons and connecting rods, a high-lift camshaft, and raised compression ratio. Its handling was praised. At one time, between 50 and 70 units a

week of the 10-h.p. were being produced. A racing Calthorpe, still with the same basic specification but with a four-speed gear-box, was capable of 85 m.p.h. in 1921.

71 MORRIS SPORTS COWLEY, 1921, Great Britain

In common with a number of other British manufacturers of modest family touring cars, William Morris in the immediately pre-First World War period offered a sports version of his standard line, the Oxford. This was a very stark two-passenger machine listed in 1914, of which few, if any, were made. Some of Morris' dealers later had the same idea: Maude's Motor Mart offered a Sports Oxford in 1918; Stewart & Arden followed suit in 1924 with a Morris Cowley; Cecil Kimber of the Morris Garages in Oxford, after beginning with sporting bodies on standard Oxford chassis in 1922, went on to sell modified cars from 1924 under the name MG (78); and Swallow, young William Lyons' concern, sold a special body on the Cowley chassis in 1927. (Until 1923, this unit was of the same dimensions as that fitted to the Oxford. 'Cowley' was merely the name of a cheaper version of the same car. From that date, the Oxford usually had a 1·8-litre engine.) From 1921 to 1924, Morris himself re-entered the field with the Sports Cowley illustrated here (though none seem to have been built after 1922). As can be seen, the normal bodywork was stark and angular, if light: the wings were aluminium. The engine was only

147

mildly tuned, but with the weight reduction, could pull a higher axle ratio than normal. In all, 107 of these cars were made.

72 AUSTIN BROOKLANDS SPORTS MODEL, 1921, Great Britain

In 1914 there appeared in the Austrian International Alpine Tour the prototype of a new sporting Austin, a successor to the 40-h.p. and 30-h.p. 'Defiance'-type (24). It was a four-cylinder side-valve of 3610 c.c. (like its 20-h.p. touring parent already in the catalogue), but the production model used a bored-out 3600-c.c. engine of 95 x 127 mm. developing 45 b.h.p. at 2000 r.p.m. After the First World War the car reappeared as a touring machine, called the Twenty, with the same basic specifications, but a sports model was retained in the range, coming in more highly tuned form ('hot' camshaft, higher compression, polished ports, larger carburettor, stronger valve springs), with better cooling, a higher axle ratio, altered suspension (including rear shock absorbers), wire wheels, and a shorter, narrower, more rounded body. This machine, illustrated here, was called the Brooklands Sports Model, after the scene of its principal successes.

73 VAUXHALL OE-TYPE, 1924, E-TYPE, 1922, Great Britain

During 1913, five examples of a new sporting Vauxhall were built beside the current C-Type or Prince Henry (24). It was initially designed to beat the all-conquering Talbot (28) and any other competition in British hill-climbs, but in fact made a habit of mopping up the opposition in speed trials and at Brooklands as well. From the beginning this E-Type was known as the '30/98' for no good reason: the R.A.C. rating was 23·8 h.p., and power output about 90 b.h.p. at 2800 r.p.m. Basically it was the same as the four-cylinder side-valve C-Type, but with a rather bigger engine (98 x 150 mm. instead of 95 x 140 mm.) giving 4½ litres and using lighter reciprocating parts (the gear-box and axles were lighter as well). The valves were bigger, and the valve timing was more 'sporting'. This engine was installed in a shorter chassis than that of the C-Type, completing a truly formidable proposition that was reliable as well as being the fastest British production car of the day, with 85 m.p.h. available. The 'Velox'-style body (upper illustration) which was standard, was light but very uncomfortable, and the brakes and chassis did not really match the performance, but after a slow start (only another eight being built before war production took over) the '30/98' became the most glamorous and desirable British sports car of the early 1920s. It could hardly be otherwise, with seventy-five wins credited to the make between 1920 and 1923, mostly credited to this model, of which only 274 were built. In 1922 it was superseded by the OE-Type, which had an engine with a shorter stroke of 140 mm. (giving 4224 c.c.) and pushrod-operated overhead valves. Power output was now 112 b.h.p. at 3300 r.p.m. but the last cars had 120-b.h.p. engines and balanced crankshafts. The OE was slightly lower-geared than the E-Type. Front wheel brakes arrived in 1923, too, and were hydraulically operated from 1926. Production ceased in 1927 after about 508 Es and OEs had been made. The lower illustration shows one of the elegant 'Wensum'-style bodies.

74 STRAKER-SQUIRE SIX
1922, 1925, Great Britain

Brazil, Straker & Co. made a very good sports car before the First World War, based on their popular four-cylinder, 3-litre, side-valve Fifteen. A new car was designed (by Roy Fedden, like the rest) during the war which was of altogether more advanced concept, based on aviation practice. There were six cylinders of 80 x 130 mm., giving 3·9 litres. They were cast separately, which was an ostensibly archaic feature, but which was thought necessary in order to achieve the precision of manufacture sought. The large overhead valves, with exposed rockers, were operated by a single overhead camshaft, and both top and bottom ends of the engine were pressure lubricated. All the reciprocating parts were very light, the pistons being aluminium. Power output was about 70 b.h.p. at 2500 r.p.m. This fine car was made at Edmonton in London by S. Straker & Squire Ltd., who sold Brazil Straker's products, as the latter had been taken over and were not interested in it. Probably between forty and sixty examples were made, between 1920 and 1925: the firm was in financial difficulties by 1923, and Sidney Straker, its driving force, died a year later. Some parts were interchangeable with one of the company's other post-war offerings, the 20-h.p., which was the bread-and-butter pre-war side-valve three-litre touring car renamed. There was also an even more obscure 1½-litre put together from proprietary bits.

75 ASTON MARTIN, 1923,
Great Britain

When he and Robert Bamford were Singer distributors before the First World War, Lionel Martin (like W. O. Bentley with the DFP) heavily modified his very touring stock-in-trade for competition purposes, and went on to construct special racing machines from other components as well. One of these gained renown at the hill-climbs held at Aston Clinton in Buckinghamshire. From 1921 (a prototype having been on the road since 1919), Martin made his own car, naming it half after himself and half after the hill. The products of Bamford & Martin Ltd were completely conventional, even conservative, in design when compared with many other sports cars, but they were beautifully (if very expensively) made in limited numbers (only about seventy in five years) for a discriminating public, and they attained a high degree of mechanical efficiency from their 1½-litre, side-valve four-cylinder engines. The engine, made by Coventry-Simplex but specially developed, united reliability with the ability to rev. freely thanks to a very robust crankshaft, lightweight pistons, and drilled connecting rods. It was also remarkably smooth-running, considering its state of tune. A four-speed gearbox was standard. High gearing combined with light, simple bodies of surpassing elegance allowed a maximum speed of at least 70 m.p.h. in the case of the most pedestrian examples, and up to 90 m.p.h. with the more highly-tuned, short-chassis version of 1922. The handling was in keeping with the performance. Some racing cars with one or two overhead camshafts and four valves per cylinder were built, and listed in 1925-6, but it is unlikely that any were sold. These more advanced machines did not have the reliability of the side-valve cars, even if they had the speed that the latter lacked in competition work. Bamford and Martin died at the end of 1925, but the car's name lived on, adorning the entirely redesigned product of a new company, Aston Martin Motors Ltd., which appeared in 1927.

76 RILEY, 1924, Great Britain

From 1919 until the end of 1928, Riley Ltd, of Coventry offered a four-cylinder car of completely conventional design, by no means cheap, rather heavy, yet of such quality and comfort that it lasted into the age of much more modern, low-priced, and efficient small cars. The 10·8-h.p. was also a good performer, for the engine could produce more power than the average 1½-litre side-valve unit of 1919, with its alloy pistons, inclined valves, and higher-than-normal compression ratio. The Riley handled well for its type, too, so it lent itself to a sporting development. This came at the end of 1922: a very pretty polished aluminium two-

passenger machine weighing only 14 cwt. that was guaranteed to reach 70 m.p.h. A four-passenger body was to be had as well. The wings on both styles were painted red from 1924, which accounted for the name of Redwing given to them. The first cars had two-wheel brakes only. The basic chassis went through several minor changes, being renamed the 11/40-h.p., and then, from 1925, the 12-h.p., when it had a bigger bore of 69 mm. instead of 66 mm., and 1645 c.c. The old 10·8-h.p. was still offered beside the newer models. At the 1926 Olympia Show, a super-sports car called the 11/50/65-h.p. was shown, but was never a production model; it used the basic engine, but with overhead valves, and a supercharger that could be disengaged.

77 ALVIS 12/50 SUPER SPORTS, 1924, Great Britain

One of Britain's finest sporting cars of the 1920s was born when T. G. John, who had taken over a design by G. P. H. de Freville that incorporated the latter's aluminium pistons, began in 1920 to produce small quantities of an expensive, high-quality light car under the name of Alvis from his Coventry works. This 10/30-h.p. performed exceptionally well, being capable of over 60 m.p.h. thanks to an engine (with side valves only) that turned out 30 b.h.p. at the high speed of 3500 r.p.m. It was not called a sports car though it was used very successfully in sporting events. The first of these came in 1922. This Super Sports wore the first example of the famous 'duck's back' body which had a horizontal pointed tail with spare wheel mounted on its underside. The original basic engine was enlarged, being renamed 11/40-h.p. and then 12/40-h.p. The latter was to be had in Super Sports form, with the indicated 40 b.h.p. Greater things were to come. The 200-mile Race at Brooklands in 1923 was won by an Alvis with a pushrod overhead-valve engine designed by Captain G. T. Smith-Clarke. A few 53-b.h.p., 90-plus-m.p.h. replicas were offered for sale, but the average sportsman was sold the Super Sports with the o.h.v. engine (initially as an option to the side-valve 12/40 unit) in a milder state of tune. This was the 12/50-h.p. unit, which from late 1924 was applied in various forms to all Alvises. Power was the indicated 50 b.h.p. or better, and while the new engine was actually quieter and smoother than the side-valve it replaced, it was still very strong and reliable. As used in the Super Sports, it was of 1496 c.c. to bring it within the $1\frac{1}{2}$-litre class in competitions, and it had a higher compression ratio, a larger carburettor, and bigger ports. The gearbox was given closer ratios than on the touring cars. In 1926, the sloping 'beetle back' replaced the 'duck's back', and that year's cars were heavier, but performance was unaltered, 75–80 m.p.h. being available. Together with the touring 12/50s, the sports car was dropped at the end of 1929, giving way to a range consisting exclusively of more refined six-cylinder cars and very fierce front wheel drive competition machines. But the 12/50 had to be reintroduced a year later, the lack of a

truly popular model in the range being acutely felt, and in spring 1931 the last sports car based on the chassis, the sports version of the 12/60, was announced. It was current in modified TL 12/60 form through 1932.

78 MG SUPER SPORTS, 1925, Great Britain

When in 1924 he began to sell modified examples of the bread-and-butter middle-class touring cars that he handled, giving them a little more performance, better roadholding qualities, the same servicing and spares facilities, and far more attractive lines at greater expense, Cecil Kimber, General Manager of the Morris Garages in Oxford, was applying principles that were far from new. Indeed, William Morris himself had made a sporting version of his own car briefly, in 1921–2 (71) and so had other Morris dealers. The initials MG that formed the name of Kimber's by-product were derived from those of his firm. He used the normal 1·8-litre Morris Oxford engine altered in respect of alloy pistons and connecting rods and polished ports, obtaining 35 b.h.p., but his lightweight aluminium coachwork, by Carbodies, was exclusive to him. (In fact, for Kimber sporting bodies had come before any other changes: he had been fitting them to Morris chassis since 1922.) Over 60 m.p.h. was available on the special high axle ratio. Kimber improved on Morris in other ways, too, standardizing vacuum servo-operated brakes earlier. Most of these 14/28-h.p. MG Super Sports were open four-passenger or two-passenger tourers, but a curiously-shaped Salonette sedan (illustrated below) was also listed. All wore the rounded Morris 'bullnose' radiator until 1927, when Morris adopted a flat configuration and Kimber did the same. For no special reason, the 1928 model and its successor of 1929, the last year of production, was called the 14/40-h.p.

79 FRAZER NASH FAST TOURER, 1925, Great Britain

After a memorable partnership making the effective but now outdated GN cycle-car (27), H. R. Godfrey and 'Archie' Frazer-Nash parted, the latter to make cars on his own, under his own name. After a couple of false starts (installing French Ruby engines in GN chassis; selling the shaft-driven Deemster car with his own radiator and body), the first classic Frazer Nash appeared in 1924. It incorporated the (now archaic) chain drive for each forward speed, gear-change by dog clutches, differential-less rear axle, direct steering, harsh suspension and stark bodies of the GN, together with its excellent power-to-weight ratio and fine handling qualities; but improved on its inspiration (and followed fashion) by utilizing a water-cooled, four-cylinder engine. The latter was a proprietary unit, at first a Plus-Power and then, from 1925, an Anzani. This was a reliable and solid side-valve unit, not capable of much improvement, but producing enough power (between 38 and 52 b.h.p. at 4000–4500 r.p.m. according to the state of tune) to give

the Frazer Nash better acceleration than most other cars on the road irrespective of size. Even so, the Boulogne Vitesse model could be had supercharged late in 1927. The type illustrated is the Fast Tourer, the least sporting, and uncomfortable, of the range in 1925. Front-wheel brakes were optional from late 1924, as were four speeds from early 1927. The latter were standard a year later. The last Anzani-engined cars were delivered in 1932, by which time between 140 and 150 had been made.

80 BAYLISS-THOMAS 10/20 h.p., 1924, Great Britain

The Excelsior Motor Company of Birmingham, who made the Bayliss-Thomas car in small numbers but highly confusing variety and nomenclature from 1922 to around 1926, built what were basically light touring cars from proprietary parts. From late 1922 at least three of these could be had with attractive long-tailed doorless aluminium sports bodies: the 1074-c.c. overhead-valve 8 h.p. with Meadows engine and Wrigley gear-box (or 9/19-h.p. as it was called in 1924): the 10·8-h.p. side-valve (renamed the 12/22-h.p. in 1923); and the 1924 10/20-h.p. illustrated here. The earlier cars such as these had quarter-elliptic springs and lacked a differential, and all Bayliss-Thomases except the 13/30-h.p. of 1924–6, which was not so much a light car as a full-scale, 1·8-litre family tourer, had three-speed gear-boxes. They were all undistinguished machines, typical of their breed.

81 ABC SUPER SPORTS,
1925, Great Britain

The products of ABC Motors of Walton-on-Thames were unusual in using air-cooled engines—in their case a 1·2-litre (later 1·3-litre) overhead-valve flat-twin designed by Granville Bradshaw. The initials stood for All-British Engine Company, makers of the power unit. The ABC car was made for nine years (between 1920 and 1929) in what were quite considerable quantities for a modest British light car manufacturer, about 1500 in all. Until 1924, the engine was of 'square' dimensions (91·5 x 91·5 mm., 1203 c.c.). Ball and roller bearings were used throughout, and the valve gear was exposed. The latter was liable to disintegrate, which was one of several failings of the car. The cylinders were at first of steel, and were of unequal expansion, with consequent engine noise, vibration and loss of power. Generally, the quality of materials was poor, which was a pity as the little car was a fierce performer in its class, 35 b.h.p. being available at 3500 r.p.m. for a weight of only 12 cwt. Its steering and road-holding qualities were also above average. The cars of 1925 and later were improved, in that the cylinders were now cast iron, the valve gear was enclosed, better lubricated and less likely to shed itself, and the crankshaft was stiffer. This was as well, as the Super Sports model (now, in common with the other models, with a bore of 96 mm. and a capacity of 1320 c.c.) turned out 40 b.h.p. This car had two carburettors, and its capabilities (50 m.p.h. in third gear, 65-plus m.p.h. in top, and an acceleration time from rest to 50 m.p.h. of 15 seconds or better)

meant that it could out-run most other cars of its type on the road.

82 BENTLEY SUPER SPORTS, SPEED MODEL, 1926, Great Britain

Britain's most famous sports car of the middle and later 1920s had modest enough beginnings; but the machine that first emerged from a mews workshop off Baker Street in London in 1919 was far from modest itself. Most small manufacturers starting up just after the First World War were content to assemble other people's standard bits, which, since they were made to suit a wide market, were usually of simple and conventional design. The more ambitious were wise to have behind them the resources of a Hispano-Suiza (39) or a Bugatti (e.g. 46). Walter Owen Bentley was different; he set out to prove that a going concern making only expensive sporting machines of advanced design could be built up from scratch. His aim was to make five such vehicles a week. His interest in sports cars went back before the war, when (being the British *concessionaire* for the French D.F.P.) he tuned one of these very pedestrian two-litre vehicles to the extent that it could finish fifth against formidable opposition in the 1914 Tourist Trophy race, and was put into small-scale production. He was one of the pioneers of aluminium pistons, which were found in this car. During the war Bentley designed aero engines (BR1, BR2). With the design collaboration of F. T. Burgess, who had been responsible for the 1914 Tourist Trophy

Humbers (themselves copies of the twin-o.h.c. Grand Prix Peugeots), he put all this experience to use. The Three Litre Bentley appeared in proto-type form in 1919, though it was not in production until 1921. Indeed, in those two years only two cars had been built—some measure of the problems Bentley had set himself. Because his resources were so small, the early Bentleys were all put together from components made by others (but to his design; be it noted that these were not proprietary parts). Aero engine practice showed itself not only in the efficiency of the design (single shaft-driven over-head camshaft operating four valves per cylinder, aluminium pistons) but also in its strength and reliability. Care on this side was shown by the provision on production cars of twin oil pumps, and twin magnetos. The recommended body styles were light, and so was the chassis, so with a power output of 80 b.h.p. at 3500 r.p.m., full use could be made of the high gearing and close gear ratios. The Three Litre carried a guarantee of 80 m.p.h. Front-wheel brakes came in 1924. The car went through a number of permutations. Since the engine was flexible as well as powerful, it was to be had from 1923 in a longer chassis with detuned engine and lower gear ratios, designed for more formal bodies. (In fact Bentley found greater demand for such a 'comfortable' chassis than for the normal spartan affair; hence the intro-duction, too, of the Big Six in 1925.) After a Bentley team finished intact in the 1922 Tourist Trophy Race, a little-known T.T. Replica was offered, with a higher compression ratio and 90 m.p.h. From 1924 the standard sports

car, with the T.T. Replica engine with twin carburettors, was called the Speed Model, and could also reach 90 m.p.h. (lower illustration). Another incarna-tion of the Three Litre was the Super Sports or Speed 100-m.p.h. model of 1925 (upper illustration), which had a shorter chassis than the Speed Model, giving it a truncated look, a tapering radiator, an 85-b.h.p. engine, and un-certain handling. Only a handful were made. The power output of the last Speed Models was about the same. A few so-called Light Tourers were made in 1925-7. They used the Speed Model chassis length, but the detuned, 70-b.h.p. engine and lower gear ratios of the formal cars. The Three Litre was made until 1929, by which time it had long been superseded by the new $4\frac{1}{2}$-litre, for although it was no longer an exceptionally fast car, it had earned an extraordinary reputation and follow-ing among richer sporting drivers, thanks mainly to wins in the Le Mans 24-hour Races of 1924 and 1927. In all, rather over 1600 Three Litres of all types were made.

83 **SUNBEAM THREE LITRE SUPER SPORTS,** 1926, Great Britain

Although the catalogue models in the Sunbeam range towards the end of 1925 were without exception the beautifully-made, very staid touring cars on which their manufacturer de-pended, the latter had a sporting reputation which at that time was second to none among British firms. Racing Sunbeams had won the 1912

Coupe de *L'Auto* Race, the 1914 Tourist Trophy, the 1923 French Grand Prix (the premier event in the calendar), the 1924 Spanish Grand Prix, and other contests of international status. The make had taken the World's Land Speed Record no less than three times. From time to time, mildly sporting versions of the standard tourers had been listed. So, it was not surprising that a serious sports car of new design should be announced in the spring of 1924, and be entered for the 1925 24-hour Race at Le Mans, in which it came a very creditable second. This machine, the Three Litre Super Sports, put into production late that year, had a most advanced specification as far as the engine was concerned, with its two overhead camshafts, two carburettors and dry sump lubrication. Power output was about 90 b.h.p. at 3800 r.p.m., giving upwards of 85 m.p.h. This unit was a road-going derivation of the successful 1923 Grand Prix engine designed by Bertarione. The car's weak point was its chassis, which broke on the Le Mans car. It was similar to that of the touring 16/50-h.p., and was too flexible for competition work. Neither were its cantilever rear springs appropriate to its use. This extremely handsome machine was usually seen with open four-paseenger bodies, but a short fabric Weymann sedan was also made. Servo-assisted brakes came in 1928. The model was offered until 1929, being available Cozette-supercharged in that year, with 140 b.h.p. and over 90 m.p.h. on tap. Around 250 Three Litres were made before a decline in the maker's fortunes and economic depression killed it.

84 SPEIDEL 8CV,
1919, 1920, Switzerland

Paul Speidel of Geneva was known for sporting *voiturettes* of the lightest kind. The first (1915–16) had an 8 CV four-cylinder Chapuis-Dornier engine; but the post-First World War Speidels were powered by M. V. (Muller-Vogel) units, also 8 CV. The upper illustration shows a type of 1918–19, with a three-speed gear-box, of which only one was made, but the production cars were rare in their class in having a four-speed gear-box (lower illustration). Maximum speed was around 56 m.p.h., which was creditable for 1920. About a dozen of these sporting *voiturettes* were made. A racing car with a 620-c.c. M.V. vee-twin engine followed in 1922, for the Swiss Grand Prix. It could reach 74 m.p.h. and could turn at no less than 6500 r.p.m. This was the last Speidel built. Paul Speidel also made motor-cycles under the name 'Quick'.

85 MERCEDES 28/95 PS,
1922, 1924, Germany

In 1914, the spectacular 37/95 PS Mercedes (see under 37/90 PS, No. 19), the most glamorous sporting car in the Daimler Motoren Gesellschaft's range, was superseded by a more modern and efficient design. This 28/95 PS, illustrated here, had a smaller engine of 7200 c.c., and although it produced its maximum power at almost equally modest revolutions (1800 r.p.m.), the output was much the same, at 95 b.h.p. The engine was more up-to-date in that it had six steel cylinders with welded steel water jackets, and its overhead valves were actuated by an overhead camshaft. Daimler's work in aero engines was reflected in this unit, as it was in the 1913 and 1914 Grand Prix Mercedes; in fact, the 28/95 PS derived directly from the 1913 G.P. cars. Maximum speed was around 78 m.p.h., and the type was current for three years after the war. In 1921, Roots-supercharged Mercedes were first catalogued. Since 1915, superchargers had been used in Daimler aero engines to enhance their high-altitude performance. The Mercedes thus became the first serious production supercharged machine, and the first make (because it was a world-famous one) to bring forced induction into prominence. It was intended in the Mercedes case primarily to improve the somewhat lethargic performance of the normal, heavy touring product; though naturally it did the same for the 28/95 PS, and gained more renown thereby, since this was the car the public knew. In 1921, a short chassis unsupercharged 28/95 PS won the Coppa Florio race in Sailer's hands, and came second in the Targa Florio. Sailer was a brave man; the Sicilian circuit was rough and tortuous, and the road-holding and brakes of the 28/95 PS were not really up to its performance even when running unblown. Apart from forced induction, the car underwent few changes during its career. The post-war car had a monobloc engine (instead of two blocks of three cylinders), and in 1923 front-wheel brakes arrived, not before time. Other victories of the 28/95 PS included the 1921 Italian Alpine Cup, and a win at the 1924 San Sebastian meeting.

86 FAFNIR TYP 471, 1923, Germany

The name of Fafnir (the dragon that guarded the Nibelungs' treasure, in German mythology) was first applied to engines that the Aachener Stahlwarenfabrik made for other motor manufacturers from 1904. The first complete cars they built appeared four years later, and until war came, these were purely touring machines of modern specification. The car illustrated was a very much fiercer proposition, the Typ 471 of 1922. The four-cylinder, overhead-valve, two-litre engine was rated at 8/50 PS, but this power output could be increased to 80 b.h.p. in supercharged form when it was called the 471K (for *kompressor*). The Zoller-blown Fafnir was the car in which the celebrated Rudolf Caracciola began his racing career. Experiments were conducted with the Zoller two-stroke engine, but no cars were made after 1926. There were Adex-type diagonally-compensated four-wheel brakes on the 471 from the beginning, and dual ignition was an option. Maximum speed in 471K form was 87 m.p.h.

87 STOEWER D10, D12, 1924, Germany

The products of Emil and Bernhard Stoewer had been associated with motor sport before the First World War (which was the Stettin firm's heyday), but afterwards, they seemed to be making a strong comeback with their D-series cars, starting in 1921, and were employing 2500 people by 1924. These were machines of conservative design with separate gear-boxes and fixed cylinder heads as late as 1926-7. The Typ D3, a 2·1-litre tourer, developed into the handsome, short-chassis sports D10, with a larger bore of 83 mm. instead of 75 mm., that was current from 1923 to 1926. The side-valve 2·6-litre four-cylinder engine developed 50 b.h.p. at 2400 r.p.m., with two carburettors. Front-wheel brakes came in 1925. In 1922 there had appeared the Typ D5, which had six cylinders with the same bore and 3·1 litres, but was otherwise very similar. Power output was only 36 b.h.p. at 2000 r.p.m., but the car was then to be seen first in D9 form (1924) and then as the D12 (lower illustration) with 45 b.h.p. The D12V had front-wheel brakes. The D10 was the more popular sports Stoewer, being faster (up to 75 m.p.h.) and won its class in the Fanoe Speed Trials of 1922, but the D12 won the 1924 Russian Reliability Trial, with a D9 second. The series was made until 1927, but by this time the firm was trying to compete with American imports by offering the same kind of car at a higher price, with predictable results.

88 NAG C4b, 1924, Germany

NAG made a notable name in competitions before 1914 (18), and preserved it after peace came. As became a business concern, however, the bread-and-butter line consisted of exceedingly solid family tourers, the relevant one here being the 10/30 PS C4 of 1920. It was a side-valve 2½-litre four of retrograde design, like so many of its contemporaries; but in 1921-2 some competition variants were triumphant on the Berlin Avus circuit, and a sports type was henceforth catalogued. This was the C4b, which produced 45 b.h.p. at 2700 r.p.m., but was called the 10/40 PS. It was very good-looking, thanks to its low lines (helped by underslung rear springs), wire wheels and outside exhaust pipes. The maximum speed of the production model was quoted at 'over 60 m.p.h.', and was in fact nearer 75 m.p.h. The axle ratio was raised. The C4b was not only faster than anything else in its class in Germany (works versions being capable of 84 m.p.h.), but it retained the reliability of its stodgy middle-class parent, as was proved when it did well in the Russian Reliability Trials of 1923 and the Reich Trials of 1923 to 1926, and when one circulated for 24 hours at 66 m.p.h. on the Monza circuit in 1924, winning its class in the Gran Premio della Notte in the hands of Christian Riecken and Hans Berthold. These two, plus Zerbst, had been the successful drivers at the Avus. Arising from this adventure, the C4b acquired the name 'Monza'. A C4b was second in the 1926 German Grand Prix, behind Caracciola in the two-litre, supercharged eight-cylinder Mercedes, but only 3½ minutes behind, in spite of tyre trouble. Production ended in the same year.

89 STEIGER SPORT, 1924, Germany

Walter Steiger was very unusual among German manufacturers in that he concentrated his efforts upon expensive sports cars—i.e. upon a minority market—and never had a line of bread-

and-butter touring cars backing them up. Paul Henze, his designer, who had worked for Cudell, RAF, and Imperia and was later to be responsible for the equally exciting Simson Supra and for a vee-eight for NAG, produced his first offering, the 10/50 PS, in 1920. The indicated brake horsepower was developed at 2500 r.p.m. It was superbly made, and extremely modern in all respects except the very long stroke. The 2·6-litre, four-cylinder engine had a shaft-driven overhead camshaft and incorporated aluminium pistons and tubular connecting-rods. Production cars were capable of about 72 m.p.h. There was also a three-litre sports car, shown here, with a bigger bore (76 mm. instead of 72 mm.), a highly-tuned engine, a short chassis and 80 b.h.p. This Steiger enjoyed considerable success in competitions in its native heath—the Avus circuit, Solitude, the Semmering hill-climb—and also ran in races abroad, notably in Italy, a favourite field for German competitors at the time, for that country nurtured less of a grudge against the defeated than the other allies of the First World War. The make was seen at Monza, and in the 1924 Targa Florio Race a Steiger was timed at 105 m.p.h., in spite of another common failing among German sports cars of the age —bad brakes. Production ended in 1926. Front-wheel brakes came only in 1925.

90 NSU 5/15 PS, 5/30 PS SPORT, 1925, Germany

NSU did not take a very great part in competitions before the First World War (4), but remedied this during the 1920s, still with the small cars for which they were best known. The development started with the modern 5/12 PS light car. This side-valve four evolved into the postwar 1·2-litre 5/15 PS and 1·3-litre 5/20 PS (5/25 PS from 1924), which were still touring machines, but in 1923 a works prepared team of 5/15s averaged nearly 75 m.p.h. for 90 miles of a race at the Avus. After this came a derivation of the 5/25 PS, the 5/30 PS Sport of 1924–6, with lightweight pistons and the indicated 30 b.h.p. and 60 m.p.h. available (though no front wheel brakes until 1926). Then appeared the even hotter, Roots-supercharged 5/25/40, producing 40 b.h.p. A $1\frac{1}{2}$-litre version won the 1925 Taunus race. The 1·6-litre 6/30 PS, a modern small six with detachable head and unit gear-box, was entered (before it went into production) in the 1926 German Grand Prix at the Avus. This was a very special supercharged version, with reduced bore to bring it into the $1\frac{1}{2}$-litre class. It won its class, and a sports version of this car, too, was offered, the supercharger being optional. So equipped, the 6/30 PS could exceed 80 m.p.h.

91 AUSTRO-DAIMLER AD617, 1921 ADV, 1923 Austria

Before the First World War, the Osterreichische Daimler Motoren Gesellschaft was world-famous for its high-performance competition cars as well as for luxury vehicles (15, 16). When peace came, middle-class touring cars had to take pride of place, as sports cars were expensive luxuries, and Austria was now a small, poor country. But since Ferdinand Porche was still in charge, something very different from the normal Germanic touring car of the period emerged from Wiener-Neustadt when a postwar range appeared. Even the basic Typ AD617, 17/60 PS Austro-Daimler that went into production in 1921 was a fast tourer rather than the customary stodgy family machine. The 4·4-litre six-cylinder engine had a single overhead camshaft, the block was aluminium, there were lightweight pistons, and the cylinder liners were steel. Once again, Porsche's aero engine experience was showing. Power output was the indicated 60 b.h.p. at 2300 r.p.m., providing a maximum speed of nearly 70 m.p.h. From 1923 to the end of production in 1926, this superbly-made car became the ADV, the suffix indicating the presence of front-wheel brakes.

92 STEYR TYP VI SPORT, 1926, Austria

The Osterreichische Waffenfabriks-gesellschaft of Steyr made their name in weapons and then in motor-cycles before they turned to car manufacture after the First World War, when guns were no longer in demand. Although an experimental vehicle had been made ten years earlier, the first Steyr cars were put into production in 1920. Hans Ledwinka, formerly of Nesselsdorf, was responsible for their design, so it is not surprising to find that these solid, rather unexciting six- and four-cylinder family tourers of the Typ II and Typ IV series had modern overhead-

camshaft engines made in unit with the gear-box (as did the prewar Nessels-dorf), and detachable cylinder heads. The Typ II of 1920-4 in normal form had a 3·3-litre engine, but it did not develop more than 40 b.h.p. at 2400 r.p.m., surprisingly in view of its ancestry. Maximum speed was just over 60 m.p.h. The Typ V was similar, except in small details. Only the Typ VI Sport of 1922-6, derived from the Typ II and illustrated here, was a sports car, though with its twin carburettors, 90 b.h.p. at 3000 r.p.m. (later 100 b.h.p.) 85-90 m.p.h. and front-wheel brakes, it was a pretty formidable one. The engine was basically the Typ II bored out to 88 mm. from 80 mm., providing 4014 c.c. This Steyr, which, with a longer-stroke, 4·9-litre engine, came third in the Targa Florio Race of 1923, was sold in Britain as the Alpine (the name Steyr not being mentioned, so as to hide the Austrian, i.e. former enemy origin of the car).

93 TATRA TYP 11, 1925, Czechoslovakia

The name Tatra is indissolubly linked with that of Hans Ledwinka, who was responsible for the design of the revolutionary cars turned out by the Tatra Werke AG and its successors from 1923 onwards. In fact Ledwinka already had a reputation for being well in advance of his time before the first Tatra was designed; prior to the First World War, when he worked for Nesselsdorf, he was making shaft-driven overhead-camshaft monobloc engines made in unit with their gear-boxes, a pattern which he took to

Steyr when peace came (92). He returned to his old firm, which now bore the Tatra name, to produce something even more surprising, and utterly different. The Typ 11 4/12 PS Tatra was powered by an 1100-c.c. horizontally-opposed, two-cylinder, overhead-valve engine developing 14 b.h.p. at 2000 r.p.m., built in unit with a four-speed gear-box and installed in the front of a tubular backbone frame with swing-axle and transverse-spring rear suspension. The Typ 12 of 1926 was identical, but for front-wheel brakes. The model was current until 1929, by which time no less than 25,000 had been made. All-up weight of the two-passenger tourer was only about 13 cwt. Two cars (of the kind illustrated here) competed in the 1925 Targa Florio Race, taking the first two places in their class in the hands of Huckel and Sponer. They differed from the production car in having swing-axle front as well as rear suspension instead of the normal transverse spring alone, and in using three valves per cylinder (two inlets, one exhaust) instead of two. Another Tatra won the 1925 Leningrad-Moscow Trial, and the model also competed in the International Alpine Trial. The Typ 11, a cheap economy car for a mass market, had little power, reaching 50 m.p.h. in standard form, but relied on its superior handling for its successes.

94 MÉTALLURGIQUE, 1922, Belgium

L'Auto Métallurgique S.A. of Marchienne-au-Pont was best known before 1914 for high-performance

sporting machinery of quite advanced design, from the 100-b.h.p. 60/80-h.p. of 1906, with overhead inlet valves, through the 95-b.h.p. 40-h.p. of 1908–13 to the 26–h.p., a five-litre machine with 75 b.h.p. in sports form that was continued from 1912 to 1923. The last new design was a two-litre, four-cylinder fast tourer in the French tradition current from the Brussels Show of 1922 to the end of the company (acquired part by Minerva and part by Imperia) in 1927. This was the car for which the firm was best known after the First World War, but it was not a true sports car, whereas its three-litre stablemate, illustrated here, very definitely was. Both were designed in 1921 by Paul Bastien, initially for the Soméa concern of Brussels in which Métallurgique had an interest. When Soméa went out of business, the machines were taken over by Métallurgique, though the man responsible for them went to work for Stutz in America. The three-litre was strictly a competition car. In 1922 it achieved 87 m.p.h. in the Oostmalle speed trials, and in the same year made the fastest lap in the Belgian Grand Prix at Spa. Its design was basically similar to that of the two-litre, with its four cylinders, single shaft-driven overhead camshaft, four-speed gear-box and Adex diagonally-compensated four-wheel brakes; but the three-litre had four valves per cylinder.

95 IMPERIA-ABADAL, 1922, Belgium

Automobiles Imperia of Liège offered only solid, stolid touring cars until

1913. In that year Señor Abadal, the firm's representative in Spain, suggested that they should make a machine like the Alfonso XIII Hispano-Suiza, one of the most famous sports cars of the era (10). In inspiring the foreign firm who supplied him to introduce a fast car, Abadal was acting much as Emil Jellinek, Austrian Consul at Nice, did when he persuaded Daimler to build the Mercedes a dozen years earlier. In fact the new car, called the Imperia-Abadal, was a carbon copy of the Hispano, and before 1914 was only made in Spain. After the First World War, with Imperia under the Van Roggen régime, other models bore the same name, one of them an extremely handsome new sports car for Belgium (illustrated here) with a long-stroke, four-cylinder three-litre engine, a single overhead-camshaft actuating four large valves per cylinder, and a maximum speed of nearly 90 m.p.h. This advanced machine, in the hands of Baron de Tornaco, won the first Belgian Grand Prix at Spa (for which race the type was originally built) in 1922, averaging 55 m.p.h. for the 375 miles, but went out of production the following year. Later Imperia sports models were little more than 'hotted-up' touring cars, though one won its class at Spa in 1925.

96 EXCELSIOR ALBERT I, 1926, Belgium

The Société des Automobiles Excelsior of Saventhem fielded some exciting cars before the First World War, notably the six-cylinder 20/30-h.p. with overhead exhaust valves (that was derived from the 85 x 130-mm., $4\frac{1}{2}$-litre, side-valve Type Adex, the basic Excelsior model from 1911 on). A racing version came eighth in the 1913 French Grand Prix, and the make was much in evidence in the 1911 Coupe de L'Auto Race and Grand Prix. After peace came, fierce sports cars were out, the company concentrating its efforts on a pure luxury machine. This new Type Adex had six cylinders too, with the same dimensions, but it had an overhead camshaft and diagonally-compensated front-wheel brakes bearing the same type name as the car. The Albert I Excelsior of 1922 (named after the King of the Belgians) was a vehicle in the same class as the H6 Hispano-Suiza (39) and the Isotta-Fraschini (69). The engine was at first 4768 c.c. and then, with a bigger bore, 5350 c.c.; it had large valves and light-weight pistons, and the brakes were servo-assisted. The sports model shown here was fitted with three carburettors and a higher axle ratio, and was capable of 105 m.p.h. by the end of its life, in spite of weighing two tons. There were three forward speeds only. Unfortunately, this glamorous car, which had no bread-and-butter line to back it up, faced too powerful competition in world markets, and could not sell in a very small home market. Its makers vanished in 1927, but not before it had more than earned its place in any history of sports cars, taking second place in the 1926 Belgian Grand Prix at Spa and winning it in the following year. On the latter occasion, it averaged 57 m.p.h. for the 24 hours. The normal luxury car produced 110 b.h.p., and the sports 130 b.h.p.

INDEX

Make	Model	Ref. No. (colour)	Page No. (text)
ABC	Super Sports 1925	81	7, 153
Alfa Romeo	RLSS 1925, 1927	68	145
Alvis	12/50 Super Sports 1924	77	150
Amilcar	Type CC 1923	43	133
Ansaldo	Tipo 4CS 1923	63	143
Apollo	Typ F Rekord 1913	21	121
Aston Martin	1923	75	149
Audi	Alpensieger 1914	22	121
Austin	Defiance 1912	25	123
Austin	Brooklands Sports Model 1921	72	148
Austro-Daimler	Prince Henry 1914	15	116
Austro-Daimler	AD617 1921, ADV 1923	91	158
Ballot	2LS 1924	45	134
Ballot	2LTS 1926	56	139
Bayliss-Thomas	10/20 h.p. 1924	80	152
Benjamin	P2 1923, Bol d'Or Type 1925	41	8, 132
Bentley	Super Sports Speed Model 1926	82	153
Benz	Prince Henry 1908, 1910	2	109
Bignan	1922	36	130
BNC	1923	42	133
Brasier	TC4 1923, 1924	40	132
Bugatti	Type 13 1910, 1914	17	118
Bugatti	Five Litre 1913	20	120
Bugatti	Brescia Type 23 1922	37	130
Bugatti	Type 30 1924, 1925	46	135
Calthorpe	Sporting Four, Super Sports 1920	70	147
Ceirano	Tipo CS 1921	61	142
Ceirano	Tipo N150S, Tipo N150 1925	66	144
Chenard-Walcker	Type X 1924, 1925	47	135
Chenard-Walcker	1926	57	140
Chiribiri	Milano, Monza Normale 1925	65	144
Cottin et Desgouttes	1911	6	3, 112
Cunningham	1919–20	31	127
Dalila	1922	38	131
Diatto	Tipo 20 1925	67	145
D'Yrsan	1924, 1927	48	136

Make	Model	Ref. No. (colour)	Page No. (text)
EHP	Le Mans 1925–26	54	138
Excelsior	Albert I 1926	96	161
Fafnir	Typ 471 1923	86	156
Fiat	Tipo 501S 1924	64	143
Frazer Nash	Fast Tourer 1925	79	152
GM	Le Mans 1925	53	138
GN	1913, 1920	27	125
Grégoire	13/18 CV 1911, 14/24 CV 1913	7	112
Hinstin SUP	1921	34	129
Hispano-Suiza Alfonso XIII	1914, 1911	10	4, 114
Hispano-Suiza	H6 1922, H6C 1926	39	131
Horch	18/22 PS 1908	1	109
Impéria-Abadal	1922	95	160
Isotta-Fraschini	Tipo KM 1912, 1914	8	6, 113
Isotta-Fraschini	Tipo 8ASS 1926	69	146
Kissel	6–55 1924, 8–75 1927	32	128
Lanchester	Sporting Forty 1914	29	126
Lorraine-Dietrich	15 CV Sport 1925, 1926	55	139
Lozier	50 h.p. 1913, 1910	12	115
Majola	Type DT 1925	49	136
Marguerite	Type BO 1925	50	136
Mercedes	37/90 PS, 16/45 PS 1913	19	120
Mercedes	28/95 PS 1922, 1924	85	155
Mercer	Type 35R 1911, Type 35J 1913	13	115
Métallurgique	Three Litre 1922	94	160
MG	Super Sports 1925	78	151
Morgan	Grand Prix 1915	30	147
Morris	Sports Cowley 1921	71	127
NAG	Typ K5 1912, 1914	18	119
NAG	C4b 1924	88	157
NSU	10/30 PS 1912, 10/28 PS 1909	4	111
NSU	5/15 PS, 5/30 PS Sport 1925	90	158

Make	Model	Ref. No. (colour)	Page No. (text)
Opel	8 PS 1909	3	110
Ratier	1926	58	140
Riley	1924	76	150
Rolls-Royce	London–Edinburgh 1911, 1913	23	121
Rolls-Royce	Continental 1913, Alpine Eagle 1914	26	124
Salmson	Grand Sport 1926, 1927	60	141
Sandford	1924–25	44	134
SCAP	6 CV 1926, 1927	59	141
Sénéchal	1921, 1925	35	129
Sizaire-Naudin	1908	5	111
Soriano-Pedroso	6/8 CV 1920	33	128
SPA	25 h.p. Sport 1913	9	113
SPA	1921, 1922	62	142
Speidel	8 CV 1919, 1920	84	155
Stanley	Gentleman's Speedy Roadster 1907, 1908	11	114
Steiger	Sport 1924	89	157
Steyr	Typ VI Sport 1926	92	159
Stoewer	D10, D12 1924	87	156
Straker-Squire	Six 1922, 1925	74	149
Stutz	Bearcat 1914, 1921	14	116
Sunbeam	Three Litre Super Sports 1926	83	154
Talbot	Competition 1914	28	125
Talbot	Type 2SC, DC 1925	52	137
Tatra	Typ 11 1925	93	159
Vauxhall	Prince Henry 1913, 1912	24	122
Vauxhall	OE-Type 1924, E-Type 1922	73	148
Voisin	Typ C5 1925	51	137